QUICKSILVER
A Hundred Years of Coaching
1750-1850

BY R. C. ANDERSON

History of Royal Blue Express Services
(with G. G. A. Frankis)

QUICKSILVER

A Hundred Years of Coaching
1750-1850

R. C. and J. M. ANDERSON

David & Charles : Newton Abbot

0 7153 6083 3

Set in 11/13pt Baskerville
and printed in Great Britain
by W J Holman Limited Dawlish
for David & Charles (Holdings) Limited
South Devon House Newton Abbot Devon

CONTENTS

LIST OF ILLUSTRATIONS

PLATES

IN TEXT

MAP

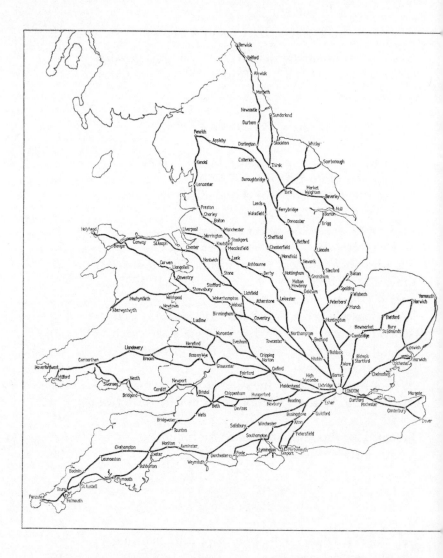

Mail coach routes from London—May 1807. Inter-working with these coaches (but not shown on this map) were 'cross road mail coaches', daily horse posts, and foot messengers. The area between Portsmouth and Dover was served by daily horse posts with the exception of the road between Portsmouth and Brighton which has a 'cross road mail coach'. The map is based on an original in the Post Office historical records department

INTRODUCTION

QUICKSILVER was chosen for the title of this book in honour of the only named Royal Mail coach, the London–Exeter–Devonport–Falmouth (Quicksilver) Royal Mail. In 1837 it became the fastest long-distance mail in the country, maintaining an average speed of 10¼mph between London and Devonport and running the 176 miles between London and Exeter in 16hr 34min, including halts for meals, change of horses, and Post Office business. Guards changed at Exeter but five coachmen would have been involved on the through journey, changing at intervals of approximately 50 miles. Put on the road in 1835 between London and Devonport it was subsequently extended to Falmouth. With the coming of the railways its route was gradually shortened until its final route was from Plymouth to Falmouth via Truro on which it made its final journey on 15 May 1859. Due to its fame certain other coaches carried its name from time to time and during 1842 there was a Quicksilver mail coach running between Falmouth and Exeter via Launceston. One of the actual Quicksilver coaches built by Vidler (and run by Charles Ward) still exists and is on display in the Museum of Transport, Kingston-upon-Hull.

In following the trail of the coaches we have travelled over many of the old routes and visited a number of the old inns, where all the hustle and bustle of coaching took place. What a network it was, and in the golden era developed a standard of service and punctuality which no system of transport by land, sea, or air has been able to approach, let alone emulate. Not for nothing was 'As right as the mails' the yardstick of the time in relation to reliability.

ROY AND JOY ANDERSON

Exeter

CHAPTER ONE

PRELUDE

'THE COACHMAN mounts to the box, Mr Weller jumps up behind, the Pickwickians pull their coats round their legs and their shawls over their noses, the helpers pull the horse-cloths off, the coachman shouts out a cheery "All right", and away they go. They have rumbled through the streets, and jolted over the stones and at length reach the wide and open country. The wheels skim over the hard and frosty ground; and the horses bursting into a canter at a smart crack of the whip, step along the road as if the load behind them: coach, passengers, cod-fish, oyster barrels, and all; were but a feather at their heels. They have descended a gentle slope, and enter upon a level, as compact and dry as a solid block of marble, two miles long. Another crack of the whip, and on they speed, at a smart gallop: the horses tossing their heads and rattling the harness, as if in exhilaration at the rapidity of the motion... A few small houses scattered on either side of the road, betoken the entrance to some town or village. The lively notes of the guard's key-bugle, vibrates in the clear cold air, and wakes up the old gentleman inside, who, carefully letting down the window-sash halfway, and standing sentry over the air, takes a short peep out, and then carefully pulling it up again, informs the others inside that they're going to change directly; on which the other inside wakes himself up, and determines to postpone his next nap until after the stoppage...

'And now the bugle plays a lively air as the coach rattles through ill-paved streets of a country town and the coachman, undoing the buckle which keeps his ribands together, prepares to throw them off the moment he stops... Mr Winkle, who sits at the extreme edge, with one leg dangling in the air, is nearly precipitated into the street, as the coach twists round the sharp corner by the cheesemonger's shop and turns into the market-place; and before Mr Snodgrass, who sits next to him, has recovered from his alarm, they pull up at the inn yard, where the fresh horses, with cloths on, are already waiting. The coachman throws down the reins and gets down himself, and the other outside passengers drop down also: except those who have no great confidence in their ability to get up again: and they remain where they are, and stamp their feet against the coach to warm them.'

So Charles Dickens described a journey of the Telegraph at the height of the coaching era during the first half of the nineteenth century. Before this heyday was reached, many centuries had passed during which the three components of public transport, a need, a vehicle and its motive power, and a way, had evolved.

Foreshadowing events of hundreds of years later the Romans established government posting stations, where light carriages, post horses, and postillions were available for persons travelling on official business. Roadside inns were provided for their refreshment and accommodation. In AD 407 the Romans left our shores and the fine road system they had created fell into disrepair. Those persons who had to travel did so on horseback or by water, goods were conveyed by pack horses, in some cases to the nearest river port where the goods were transferred into barges. During the Middle Ages road repair and maintenance became the responsibility of some of the richer monasteries, but where they failed to do this there was no law, system, or custom to attend to the roads. The Statute of Winchester, passed in 1285, attempted to clear the woods and the surrounding vegetation either side to a depth of 200ft, so that robbers could not lay in wait for travellers. But statute without a system could not put matters right, and during the thirteenth and fourteenth centuries the large proportion of travellers were pilgrims, journeying to and from the sixty or seventy shrines dotted about England. Some carriages did exist but these were mainly for conveying goods.

Parliament passed the first Highways Act in 1555; repair of the roads then became the parish responsibility, but the Act was not enforced, the results of which are best summed up by the experience in 1600 of one William Kemp, who embarked upon a morris dance from London to Norwich. He wrote:

At length coming to a broad plain of water and mud, which could not be avoided, I fetched a rise, yet fell in over the ankles at the further end. My youth that followed me took his jump, and stuck fast in the midst.

In 1558 Elizabeth I succeeded to the throne and by 1564 she was using a carriage brought over from Holland by William Booren, who became her majesty's coachman. The early carriages were most uncomfortable vehicles and in Elizabeth's own words to the French ambassador in 1568, 'I was still suffering aching pains from being knocked about in a coach driven too fast a few days before.'

The use of carriages increased in the closing years of Elizabeth's reign and it is evident that a desire for display rather than comfort brought about their increasing use. There was a

step forward in 1593: an Act was passed establishing the mile
as 1,760 yards. A Bill proposed in 1601, as a result of the
increasing number of coaches coming into use, sought to
restrain their excessive use and forbid men riding in them,
but it did not become law. Four years later both hackney and
private coaches were in common use in London. Carters and
waggoners hated them but the primitive construction of the
coaches and the dreadful condition of the roads rendered them
virtually impossible to use in the country. Even so six horses
were in general use but the Earl of Northumberland in 1619,
goaded into the making of display with the Duke of Bucking-
ham's team of six horses, decided to have a team of eight 'and
so rode', we are told, from London to Bath, 'to the vulgar talk
and admiration' of those watching.

In 1648 one John Taylor made a journey to the Isle of
Wight, whose party hired the Southampton Coach which
came weekly to the Rose, near Holborn Bridge. His description of the journey is an historic document:

> We took our two coachmen and fourhorses,
> And merrily from London made our course,
> We wheel'd the top of th' heavy hill call'd Holborne,
> (Up which hath been full many a sinful soule borne)
> And so along we jolted past St Gileses,
> Which place from Brainford six (or neare) seven miles is
> To Stanes that night at five o'clock we coasted,
> Where (at the Bush) we had bak'd, boyl'd and roasted.
> Bright Sol's illustrious Rayes the day adorning,
> We past Bagshot and Bawwaw Friday morning.
> That night we lodg'd at the White Hart at Alton,
> And had good meate—a table with salt on,
> Next morn W'arose with blushing cheeked Auroria;
> The wayes were faire, but not so faire as Flora,
> For Flora was a goddesse and a woman,
> And (like the highwayes) to all men was Commar,
> Our horses, with the Coach, which we went into,

Page 17 The original Bath mail coach, 1784

Page 18 (above) 'All right.' The Exeter mail coach after a change of horses; (below) the Turnpike Gate (both painted by C. C. Henderson)

Coaches at this time had a wooden frame, covered with leather nailed to the frame. Windows and doors were unknown. Low hung with the heavy body slung by leather braces from the upright posts springing from the axle trees of rear and front wheels, the body motion was violent in a lateral direction but fore and aft motion was restrained. It was not therefore unknown for the body to collapse as a result of the opposing forces. Coachmen were expected to carry out roadside repairs and carried a box of tools under their seats, which were placed immediately over the front wheels. As there were no springs the effect of the violent shocks on his body transmitted from the wheels can hardly be imagined. The first coach mentioned with glazed windows was the glass coach made for the Duke of York in 1661 but vibration easily broke the windows and coach builders continued using shutters or leather curtains. By 1667–8 coaches were on hire in London and we learn of Samuel Pepys petitioning in December 1667 for arrears in his salary and expenses including a continual expense of coach hire and boat hire—arising frequently to 6s 8d and sometimes more in a day. Pepys was a regular user of coaches for business and pleasure and he writes of his amorous adventure with an actress that 'he drove with the fascinating creature in a hackney coach through the Park, after the play was done, kissing her a little tentatively'. During 1668 Pepys made a tour of England after which he decided to buy his own coach. It seems the secondhand carriage market at this time was fraught with problems not dissimilar to those experienced when purchasing a secondhand motor-car. Fortunately for Pepys he was advised by friends and, having obtained his four-seat light chariot, he resolved not to be contented with hired horses but to purchase a pair of his own. This he did at the horse market at Smithfield, purchasing for £50 a pair of black horses 'the Beautifullest almost', he thought, 'I ever saw'. It cost him £2 to replace a shattered pane of glass, which suggests that windows were becoming

more common. Private coaches were very popular in the latter
half of the century and Pepys, who became more and more the
man of fashion as his career developed, shared the pleasures
and pride of the affluent, who could afford such luxurious and
expensive items.

Although coaches were developing the roads got no better,
and when the Duke of Somerset resided at Petworth, in Sussex,
the roads were so bad it was virtually impossible to get there.
Petworth is 49 miles from London, but the duke had a house
at Godalming, 26 miles from London, where he stayed the
night. Word was always sent in advance when the duke started
his journey so that his servants could be out on the roads to
point out the holes. When the Emperor Charles VI visited
Petworth he was escorted by strong peasants to keep the coach
upright, but, despite their efforts, the coach was overturned
several times.

In 1667 a London–Oxford coach was performing the 54-
mile journey in two days and in the following year we find the
first appearance of the epithet Flying in the advertisement.

FLYING MACHINE

All those desirous to pass from London to Bath, or any
other place on the Road, let them repair to the 'Bell
Savage' on Ludgate Hill in London and the 'White Lion'
at Bath at both which places they may be received in a
Stage Coach every Monday, Wednesday and Friday.
Which performs the whole Journey in Three Days (if
God permit) and sets forth at five o'clock in the morning.
Passengers to pay one pound five shillings each, who are
allowed to carry fourteen pounds weight for all about to
pay three-halfpence per pound.

April 1669 saw a 'Flying Coach' between Oxford and London
—coach not machine, which term did not come into general
use until about seventy years later. The same year saw the

Chester stage doing the journey in six days and whilst there is no positive information it is to be assumed that coaches must have been running to other cities and on other routes about which no record has survived.

Not everyone liked the coaches and Weeping Cross outside Salisbury was the name of the place where family and friends took leave of travellers never expecting to see them again. Generally, travellers made their wills before they set out on their journeys. In 1673 John Cusset wrote:

> Will any man keep a horse for himself and another for his servant all the year round, for to ride one or two journeys, that at pleasure, when he hath occasion can slip to any place where his business lies for two or three shillings, if within twenty miles of London, and so proportionately to any part of England? No there is no man, unless some noble soul that seems to abhor being confined to so ignoble, base and sordid a way of travelling as these coaches oblige him to and who prefers a public good before his own case and advantage, that will keep horses.

Cusset considered the rigours of the journey were injurious to health and asked:

> What additive is this to men's health or business, to ride all day with strangers often times sick, or with diseased persons, or young children crying, to whose humours they are obliged to be subject, forced to bear with, and many times are poisoned with their nasty scents and crippled by the crowd of their boxes and bundles?

He did not think much to the coachman either, considering him 'surly, dogged and ill-natured'. Whilst he did not advocate the total suppression of such methods of travelling, he proposed that coaches should be limited to one for every country town in England, to go backwards and forwards once a week. There were other opponents who for a variety of reasons thought the same way, but time marches on and in 1673 the journey to Exeter is put at eight days in summer, ten in winter and, what is more important, it had become an all-the-year service. May 1677 saw the establishment of the Worshipful Company of Coach and Harness Makers and in 1678 an important cross-country link was introduced between Hull and York to connect with the York–London coach. Although summer only it connected at York with coaches to Leeds, Wakefield and other places. Municipal enterprise in 1678 saw the proposal of a weekly service between Edinburgh and Glasgow by agreement between Provost Campbell and the magistrates of Glasgow with William Hoorn of Edinburgh. Unfortunately this attempt and others failed and it was not until 1749 that the first conveyance to ply regularly between Glasgow and Edinburgh in two days was established. It was succeeded in 1759 by the Fly which brought the time down to a day and a half.

In the work of De Laune, 'The Present State of London', dated 1681, he lists all the stage coaches, carriers, and waggons to and from London in that year. Of the 119 coaches listed, 65 were on long distance routes and the remainder served points within a 25-mile radius from London. Of local services known to have centred on York and other provisional centres there is no information but such services did exist and changeover of passengers between one coach and another took place. Services of various intensity were operating to Bath, Brentwood, Bristol, Cambridge, Canterbury, Chelmsford, Exeter, Gloucester, Lincoln, Norwich, Oxford, Portsmouth, Reading, Saffron Waldon, Stamford, Ware and Windsor, although several other towns and cities were probably served by services of which there is no longer a record and inshore sea transport also provided facilities.

A change in attitude was developing, people were appreciating travel and services changed. Some ceased, other operators

CHAPTER TWO

THE FOUNDING OF A LEGEND

STAGE WAGGONS

THE STAGE waggon came into use about 1500; it was the poor man's coach and it creaked and groaned its tedious way at about two miles per hour. It was a predecessor of all public vehicles and it was thus the poor who became the first stage-coach passengers. Towards 1570 goods traffic became a permanent feature on the road and one of the sixteenth-century pioneers was Thomas Hobson, who operated a stage waggon between London and Cambridge on an exclusive basis specially licensed by the University, whose letters he conveyed. His son, who died in 1631 in his eighty-sixth year, had also a very lucrative business of letting out saddle horses. From his determination to allow no picking and choosing, and his refusing to allow any horse to be taken out of its proper turn, first arose that immortal proverb Hobson's Choice, that or none—in other words, no choice whatever.

The predecessors of the stage waggons were pack horses and as late as the first years of the nineteenth century in the North of England, the west and other extreme corners of the country the packman and his horses kept the rural districts supplied with their barest requirements. In the remote areas of Devon, where some of the old packman's ways can be traced, it is fanciful to imagine the packman with his team of horses and a talbot by his side; the talbot being the old English hound something between a foxhound and bloodhound—a fierce creature who guarded his master's property from the thieves and dangers encountered on the journey. There is an inn of the same name in Cirencester with a fine picture of one of these animals on the inn sign.

By 1750 the gradual introduction of two classes of vehicles between the common stage waggon and the stage coach had begun. First was the flying stage waggon which whilst similar in construction to the stage waggon changed horses at inns on route and therefore progressed quicker. The other type of vehicle was the caravan or long coach which resembled a gipsy van and was fitted with benches for eight, twelve and some-times eighteen passengers.

There were numerous social grades in travel at this time, but waggoners were a pleasant and light-hearted crowd if one is to believe the old English ballad:

Jolly Waggoners
It is a cold and stormy night, I'm wetted to the skin,
But I'll bear it with contentment till I get to my inn
And then I'll sit a-drinking with the landlord and his kin,
        Sing wo! my lads, sing wo!
        Drive on, my lads, gee-ho!
For who can live the life that we jolly waggoners do-o-o?

How did these humble folk eat and drink, and where did they lodge? Sometimes under the waggon and at other times the stable lofts of the inn formed their apartments. They had supper of cold boiled beef and bread in the kitchen, and slept in the hay in the loft or under the waggon at an inclusive price of 6d or 9d. Social distinction did not permit them to mix with the inside passengers from the stage coaches even if they could have afforded it.

In 1750 there were twenty-five to thirty waggons weekly, from Birmingham to London, carrying goods at from £3 to £4 per ton; thirty years earlier the cost had been £7 per ton. On the routes from the West of England the waggons were drawn by teams of eight horses, augmented by two, four or even more horses, on many of the hills over which they brought heavy goods and luggage in twelve days from Falmouth to London at a rate of three miles an hour, carrying passengers at a halfpence a mile.

With the second decade of the nineteenth century a demand arose for the quicker conveyance of goods to London, the seaports and the manufacturing towns. With the improved roads it became possible to comply and new waggons described as the fly vans appeared on the roads in the 1820s. The vans of Russel & Co, van proprietors, trading between London and the West of England, were typical. These vehicles completed the journey in the same period as the ordinary stage coaches of that period, and, running night and day, continued to set forth and come to their journey's end until the railways came and swept away the fly vans, stage coaches and mails alike. Goods from Falmouth in the 1830s left the offices of Russel & Co, at Killigrew Street, every Monday at noon and arrived at the Castle & Falcon Inn, Aldersgate Street, London, on the following Saturday. It was not unusual for a waggon to be accompanied by an armed guard if it conveyed such valuables as bullion brought by the packets to Falmouth.

As long distance waggons disappeared off the Cornish roads in the 1830s they were replaced by carriers' vans and horse omnibuses. The former conveyed both passengers and goods and plied between various parts of the country. It is the latter which is of particular interest in so far as it was a precursor of the modern bus, having longitudinal wooden seats inside the body, which had windows along the sides. Outside passengers were also conveyed. Besley's *Route Book of Cornwall*, published in the 1850s, records:

> We do not know whether Cornwall lays claim to the parentage of the omnibus family, now so common in every part of England, but we can testify to having seen vans in use for the conveyance of passengers in this county many years before they were introduced generally in London.

Many of these omnibuses obtained contracts for conveying the mails and were described as 'fast mail omnibuses'. It seems that they may well have replaced mail coaches in Cornwall, had not railway development proceeded so fast. One of the most famous of these was the Fairey which commenced in the 1850s and ran between Truro and Plymouth, later being extended to Penzance. It offered a connection at Plymouth with the railway enabling persons residing in Cornwall to travel to or from London in a day. On less frequent routes the common stage waggon and flying waggon lingered on well into the railway age. Immediately preceding railways the heavy covered goods vans were exclusively devoted to the conveyance of freight, ceasing to carry passengers. At this time two-thirds of the freight went by canal and if the railways had not come along there would undoubtedly have been a great improvement in the roads on which the main routes were becoming vastly overburdened. So the coming of the railways was perhaps provident. The Helston–Lizard horse omnibus continued until replaced in 1903 by the Great Western Railway motor-bus—the first provincial bus service in the country. The fact that Cornwall had such an extensive

network of horse omnibus services at such an early date is
of immense interest and on market days some fifty departed
from Truro alone at 5pm, the horses having been brought
from the stables at 4.30pm and harnessed to the omnibuses.
So the earliest of the public vehicles, the stage waggon (described as common stage waggons by an Act of Parliament)
was also the last until supplanted by motor vehicles. They
continued to follow their traditional routes to and from
London precisely as they had done from the beginning.

PICKFORD & COMPANY

Pickfords are the successors to the packhorse carriers, but
the original date of their entering into business is lost in the
mist of time as no records exist. By an advertisement in *Pres-
cott's Manchester Journey*, dated 4 January 1777, we become
aware of Matthew Pickford's flying waggons operating between the Swan and Saracen's Head, Market Street Lane,
Manchester, every Wednesday, journeying to the Swann Inn,
Lad Lane, London, in 4½ days. It is apparent that extensive
connecting facilities existed from Manchester to other major
towns in Lancashire. In the second decade of the nineteenth
century, under the guidance of Joseph Baxendale in succession to the Pickford brothers, the business was thoroughly
reorganised and expanded, the journey between London and
Manchester being reduced to 36 hours for 186 miles. It is
interesting to note here that Baxendale was advertising this
facility as caravan on springs and carrying guarded goods
only, every afternoon at 6pm. Eventually the picturesque
name was reduced to van—which it has been ever since.
In 1826 Baxendale opened a new head office in Gresham
Street, London. He became involved in canal traffic, and
when the Regent's Canal opened in 1820 Pickford & Co had
wharves ready.

One of the first businesses to pension employees on retire-
ment, Baxendale foresaw that railways must succeed, so he

threw in his lot with the railways, who welcomed the proposed alliance; Pickfords, with Chaplin and Horne, acquired shares in the town and country carrying agencies for those railways which, in 1845, became the London & North Western Railway.

STAGE COACHES

The eighteenth century built a way of life whose character was essentially urban. New ideas, fashions, modes of art began in the metropolis, but they travelled to the provincial cities. The need to link the towns efficiently was the driving force behind the new forms of rapid transport. The towns were where life went on, and life was as much art as it was commerce. It was no longer possible to sit and content oneself in one's village dreaming over local gossip and fantastic rumours from the unknown world outside, for the world outside was beginning to enter in person, drawn by four horses, and travel became a civilised necessity of the eighteenth century, but not everyone had their own facilities. The wealthy had their own coaches, post chaises were expensive, stage waggons were the conveyance of the poor, and so the stage coach evolved to meet the middle-class need. The concept of the stage coach was revolutionary, with its planning of journeys, staff, horses, and times of arrival at inns.

Travellers began to appreciate the new mode of travel, slowly at first, but as the routes grew more enterprising and the turnpike system developed, so need and the satisfaction of this need interacted to produce a network. Competition spurred on the development of coaches beautifully built with a mirror finish to the paintwork. The ownership rested with the contractors, who hired out their vehicles to the small operators, who put them into service. They termed themselves the proprietors, horsed and manned the coaches and kept an interest in, and control in many cases of, the inns on route. Coaches went back to contractors for regular attention. The exteriors were magnificent, with their gold, blue, whites, crimsons, the name of the proprietor and coach, together with the inns that were the terminal, prominently displayed on the panelling. It is interesting to observe the lines of development from which two themes developed—speed or comfort— and speed won.

At the beginning of the eighteenth century the coaches still had the same horses throughout the journey and travel was slow despite the fact that at 10-mile intervals, relays of saddle horses were available throughout the country. The coach operators were alive to the position but the uncertainty of passengers, the difficulty of arranging for changes at known places of call, and the fact that some coaches followed a varied route to suit the convenience of travellers were problems to be overcome before planned changes could be made. In May 1734, however, a Newcastle–London Flying Coach was commenced,

> To be performed in nine days, being three days sooner than any coach that travels the road: for which purpose eight stout horses are stationed at proper distances.

At the same time one John Dale announced that a coach would take the road from Edinburgh to London towards the end of each week in nine days. By 1754 the Edinburgh coach required ten days in summer and twelve days in winter, but it was a 'glass machine' hung on steel springs. Sunday was still a day of rest and no service was provided. To reach Edinburgh in the 1760s one had the choice of travelling on horse back, stage coach, post chaise or by sea. In 1762 James Boswell travelled up by post chaise, with overnight stops at Berwick, Durham, Doncaster and Biggleswade. It took five days and cost him £11. The journey was not without incident because on the first day one of the wheels broke, and refusing the driver's proposal that they should leave the chaise and ride the horses to Berwick, Boswell 'made the chaise be dragged on to Ayton, where we waited till the driver rode to Berwick and brought us a chaise'. It seems the temporary accommodation and food were poor. The second and third days were without incident but on the fourth 'a young unruly horse in the chaise, which run away with the driver and jumping to one side of the road, we were overturned'. Both Boswell and his companion suffered minor injuries and as both had a fear of highwaymen they each carried a loaded pistol, so we can appreciate his sentiments that 'when we came upon Highgate Hill and had a view of London, I was all life and joy'.

On the threshold of the Industrial Revolution, Britain's only alternative inland transport system to canals was the roads system and those were in the hands of unwilling, incompetent and mainly powerless men governed by statutes, that were either ineffective, conflicting, unworkable and in a large number of instances not understood by those who were supposed to abide by them. Manufacturing England was coming into existence and although Birmingham had had direct communication with London since 1679, public demand resulted in a Flying Coach commencing in 1742, followed in 1758 by an Improved Birmingham Coach. Manchester and London came into direct communication in 1754 and four years later the Liverpool Flying Machine was established to travel the $206\frac{1}{2}$ miles between Liverpool and London in three days at a fare of £2 2s. Leeds followed with a Flying Coach of 1760 routed via Barnsley, Wakefield and Sheffield.

Fowler's Shrewsbury stage coach began in June 1764 to ply to and from London in three and a half days; fare one guinea inside, outside half a guinea. If the outsiders were not carried on the roof they were carried in 'the basket', a great wicker-work structure hung by stout leather straps on the back of the coach between the rear wheels and resting on the axle tree. Originally intended to convey the luggage it was

EXPEDITIOUS TRAVELLING

FROM

LONDON TO GLASGOW AND PORTPATRICK,

IN FOUR DAYS,

BY WAY OF CARLISLE AND DUMFRIES.

A NEW POST COACH sets out from the 'CROSS KEYS,' WOOD STREET, LONDON, *every evening* (Saturday excepted), and arrives at BECK'S COFFEE HOUSE, CARLISLE, in three days; also sets out from BECK'S COFFEE HOUSE, CARLISLE, *on the same evening,* and arrives in three days at the 'CROSS KEYS,' LONDON. To accommodate passengers travelling northward and to Ireland A NEW POST COACH, which connects with the above, sets out from ' KING'S ARMS HOTEL,' CARLISLE, *every Tuesday and Thursday morning* at six o'clock for DUMFRIES; upon arrival of which at the 'GEORGE INN,' a DILIGENCE sets out for GLASGOW and another for PORTPATRICK. Also a DILIGENCE sets out from MR. BUCHANAN'S, the 'SARACEN'S HEAD,' GLASGOW, and another from MR. CAMPBELL'S, PORTPATRICK, *every Tuesday and Thursday morning* at four o'clock, to join the said DUMFRIES AND CARLISLE POST COACH, in which seats will be reserved for those travelling southward.

Each inside passenger from Carlisle to Glasgow or Portpatrick to pay £1 16s. 6d., and to be allowed ten pounds weight of luggage; all above to pay 2d. per lb. Children on the lap to pay half-price. Insides from Carlisle to Dumfries to pay 11s. 8d.; outsides, 6s. 8d. Small parcels from Carlisle to Portpatrick or Glasgow to pay 1s. 6d. each; all upwards of nine pounds to pay 2d. per pound. Passengers taken up on the road to pay 4d. per mile in both the Coach and Diligence; and for outsides on the Coach 2½d. per mile. Insides from London to Glasgow, £3 6s. Ditto from Carlisle to Glasgow or Portpatrick, £1 16s. 6d. Total: London to Glasgow or Portpatrick, £5 2s. 6d.

Fig 1 Advertisement for a 'post coach' between London, Glasgow and Portpatrick, 1779

found capable of holding passengers, who suffered much in order to ride cheaply. Outside seats had not arrived and three outside passengers sat on the front part of the roof with their feet on the driving box. Another one had a place on the box seat with the driver and a further three sat on the rear of the roof where they had nowhere to rest their feet and had the greatest difficulty in maintaining their position. Although the passengers were provided with grab handles they were of little use and there was every chance of their being thrown off the coach if it lurched.

An account of a coach journey in 1782 by Charles H. Montz shows that those who were obliged to ride cheaply endured fearful conditions totally devoid of any glamour we might associate with coaching as depicted on Christmas cards! Travelling to London Montz

Determined to take a place as far as Northampton on the outside, but the ride from Leicester to Northampton I shall remember as long as I live. The coach drove from the yard through a part of the house. The inside passengers got in from the yard, but we on the outside were obliged to clamber up in the street, because we shall have no room for our heads to pass under the gateway. My companions on the top of the coach were a farmer, a young man very decently dressed, and a blackamoor. The getting up alone was at the risk of one's life and when I was up I was obliged to sit just at the corner of the coach, with nothing to hold on by, but a sort of little handle fastened on the side. I sat nearest the wheel, and the moment we set off I fancied I saw certain death before me. All I could do was take still tighter hand hold of the handle, and to be strictly careful to preserve my balance. The machine rolled along with prodigious rapidity over the stones through the town of Leicester and every moment we seemed to fly into the air, so much so that it appeared to me a complete miracle that we stuck

Page 35 The London–
Devonport (Quicksilver)
Royal Mail coach
at the Museum of
Transport, Hull

Page 36 (above) Stage coach passengers at breakfast; (below) 'Mail.' The guard drops the mail bag off to the waiting postmistress. Note the letter box, the milk maid and two farm hands (engraved by G. Hunt)

to the coach at all. But we were completely on the wing as often as we passed through a village or went down a hill.

This continued fear of death at last became insupportable to me, and therefore, no sooner were we crawling up a rather steep hill, and consequently proceeding slower than usual, than I carefully crept from the top of the coach, and was lucky to get myself ensconced in the basket behind. 'O sir you will be shaken to death!' said the blackamoor; but I heeded him not, trusting that he was exaggerating the unpleasantness of my new situation, and truly as long as we went slowly up the hill, it was cosy and pleasant enough; and I was just on the point of falling asleep, having had no rest the night before, when on a sudden the coach proceeded at a rapid down-hill rate. Then all the boxes, in nailed and copper-fastened, began as it were to dance around me, everything in the basket appeared to be alive, and every moment I received such violent blows that I thought my last hour had come. The blackamoor had been right, I now saw clearly, but repentance was useless, and I was obliged to suffer horrible torture for nearly an hour, which seemed to me an eternity. At last we came to another hill, when quite shaken to pieces, bleeding, and sore, I ruefully crept back to the top of the coach to my former seat. 'Ah did I not tell you that you would be shaken to death?' inquired the black man, when I was creeping along on my stomach. But I gave him no reply, indeed I was ashamed; and I now write this as a warning to strangers who are inclined to ride in English stage coaches and take an outside seat, or worse still, horror of horrors, a seat in the basket.

From Harborough to Northampton I had a most dreadful journey. It rained incessantly, and as before we had been covered with dust, so now we were soaked with rain. My neighbour, the young man who sat next to me in the middle, every now and then fell asleep; and when in this

c

state he perpetually bolted and lolled against me with the whole weight of his body, more than once nearly pushing me from my seat, to which I clung with the last strength of despair. My forces were nearly giving way when at last happily, we reached Northampton, on the evening of 14 July 1782, an ever memorable day to me.

On the next morning I took an inside place for London. We started early. The journey from Northampton to the metropolis, however, I can scarcely call a ride for it was perpetual motion or endless jolt from one place to another, in a close wooden box, over what appeared to be a heap of unhewn stones and trunks of trees scattered by a hurricane. To make my happiness complete, I had three travelling companions, all farmers who slept so soundly that even the hearty knocks with which they hammered their heads against coachwork and against mine did not awake them. Their faces bloated and discoloured by ale and brandy and the knocks aforesaid, looked as they lay before me, like so many lumps of dead fish. I looked, and certainly felt, like a crazy fool when we arrived at London in the afternoon.

'What's in a name!' A great deal when one writes about coaching. The Trades Description Act did not apply and the title of a coach as a Flying Machine or Diligence did not necessarily mean that the traveller would meet such a definite mode of travel. Names again referred to the type of vehicle and others to denote a particular coach to distinguish it from its competitors on a particular road. In the early days proprietors described their vehicles quite simply as a coach or a stage coach, adding some complimentary adjective such as elegant, when a competitor came upon the scene. A further development to meet competitors was not usually to offer a better service—this was usually left to the opposition trying to push in on established ground—but to describe the coach as the original. It was not unusual for competitors to take up

the cudgels by way of press advertisements describing their
opponent's vehicle in derogatory terms—'judge whether he
won't return to his old prices when you cannot help your-
selves, and use you as formerly'.

The development of coaching varied throughout the country
and not unnaturally was more advanced on the more competitive roads where proprietors endeavoured to win traffic by
describing their coaches as Machines or Flying Machines,
terms which came into more general use after 1750, although
there had been a Flying Machine on the Bath road in 1667.
In 1773 that popular adjective of the 1970s ('new') appeared
as a trading description, and subsequently there came New
Flying Machine, which was soon renamed the New Fly. Quite
a few proprietors made the use of steel springs as a feature of
the advertisement and of course quicker time was a favourite. Going one better was the Diligence conveying three
passengers, first introduced on the Shrewsbury–London road.
Competing with two other coaches it travelled fastest at the
lowest fares, but the demand was not there and in due course
it was withdrawn. The name, however, caught on, although
proprietors were already operating post coaches and light post
coaches in general which offered faster travel than the stage
and mail coaches. Post chaises were the fastest of all and the
Diligence was very similar, and indeed the first mail coach
was of this type. The term was abused and far from describing a fast, light coach conveying three persons the title was
bestowed on numerous vehicles, some conveying six or eight
persons.

It was not only speed which put the post coaches and light
post coaches at the top of the coaching tree, but also their
expensive and limited exclusive accommodation reduced the
opportunity of travel with objectionable characters. As John
Wesley wrote:

I went to Norwich (from London) in the stage coach

with two very disagreeable companions, called a gentleman and gentlewoman, but equally ignorant, insolent,
loud, and profane.

Macready wrote similarly in 1811 of a journey by stage from
Birmingham to London:

I got onto the coach; its odours were many, various and
unpleasantly mingled, and the passengers, a half-drunken
sailor and an old woman, did not impress me with the
prospect of a very pleasant journey. The pace at which
the vehicle proceeded made me doubt whether it would
ever reach London, and its creakings and joltings seemed
to augur a certain overturn.

Apparently it took five hours to cover the 18 miles from
Birmingham to Coventry. Another category of travel was the
Accommodation coach, slow moving, stopping at frequent
intervals to take up and set down passengers, but offering
a very useful facility in many areas. To further distinguish
their coaches proprietors gave them individual names. Thus
we have True Blue running between Leeds, Malton and
Scarborough; and in 1784 the Expedition running on the
London and Norwich road, which had seen one of the earliest
named coaches in 1659—the Confatharrat, an old-time spelling of Confederate and presumably run by a confederation
of proprietors. Ballooning caught the public imagination in
1784 so in 1785 we read of the first Balloon coach and in
1784 also the first Defiance appeared on the road between
Leeds and Hull. But the roads were in such a deplorable
state that speeds could not be increased and this was the key
to the matter. The need was there and by and large the
vehicle, but the way was not. The Exeter Flying Stage pur-
ported in 1793 to perform the journey in three days, but
generally took six, and sometimes longer in the winter. Its
itinerary was:

MONDAY depart Saracen's Head, Skinner Street, Snow
Hill dines at Egham lies at Murrel's Green.

TUESDAY dines at Sutton, lies at the Plume of Feathers
in Salisbury.

WEDNESDAY dines at Blandford lies at the King's
Arms in Dorchester.

THURSDAY at one o'clock Exeter.

Illustrating the state of the roads on the Exeter road at that
time one may quote a correspondent who wrote to the *Gentlemen's Magazine*.

After the first forty-seven miles from London, [he wrote]
you never set eye on a turnpike. Dorchester is to us a
terra incognita, and the map-makers might if they pleased
fill the vicinities of Devon and Cornwall with forests,
sands, elephants, savages or what they please,

As for the country along the Exeter road it was reported to
be picturesque, but the state of the road forbade anyone
making its acquaintance. It seems that the roads in Cornwall
were somewhat better. G. B. Morgan wrote:

The two great post entrances to Cornwall are by Launceston and Tor Point; if you enter by the latter you have
to cross the harbour of Hamoaze which at times is rough
and turbulent; and the road as far as Liskeard is excessively hilly. The eastern travellers with whom I have
associated at the different inns, during my perambula-
tions, are of opinion that the roads, with some exceptions
are tolerably good throughout the county, much better
than in many parts of Devonshire. The quarterstone so
abundant in most parts of Cornwall, is an admirable
material for repairing the roads.

Coaching in Cornwall was directly linked with the Falmouth
packet service (see Chapter 8) and this gave a great stimulus

to its development in the area; another factor of great importance was the expansion of mining in Cornwall during the nineteenth century and whilst the copper, tin, coal and timbers went by sea the engineers and other interested parties travelled to and fro by coach. Some however travelled to Cornwall for pleasure—Bude was advertising its attractions in the late 1700s, and the mild climate in the far west enabled Penzance to develop as a resort from about the same time.

The first stage coach in Cornwall about which definite information is available commenced around 1790 running on alternate days between Exeter and Falmouth via Bodmin. Leaving Exeter at 3am it took twenty-two hours to complete the journey of roughly 100 miles. It soon had its competitors who appeared to prefer a more leisurely journey as they stopped at Bodmin and required two days. Timekeeping was not too precise either in the 1790s; a coachman, on being asked what time the coach would arrive in London, replied, 'That the proper time was six o'clock, but that he had been every hour of the four and twenty after it.'

A further development in communications occurred in 1790 when the ferry was regularly established by Act of Parliament across Hamoaze between Morrice Town, Plymouth Dock (present Devonport) and Mutton Cove, Torpoint, the service commencing on 4 July 1791. Following on from this Walter Cross, a Mevagissey seaman and smuggler, took an inn at Torpoint and another at Liskeard and in 1796 introduced a stage coach between Torpoint and Truro. Other inn keepers were soon off the mark, and in opposition a coach, the Prince of Wales, was established on alternate days between Torpoint and Falmouth via Truro. Lack of revenue forced the proprietors of the rival coaches to join forces but this uneasy alliance soon failed and in 1799 Mr Hooper of the King's Arms, Torpoint (one of the earlier participants), went on his own in opposition to the Prince of Wales. The new coach commenced on 21 January 1799 and is the first

authentic date for a Cornish coach. The fares charged are of
interest:

		Inside	Outside
Torpoint to Liskeard		7s 6d	3s 6d
”	” Lostwithiel	12s 0d	6s 0d
”	” St Austell	15s 6d	8s 0d
”	” Grampound	18s 6d	9s 6d
”	” Truro	£1 1s 0d	10s 6d
”	” Falmouth	£1 4s 0d	12s 0d

Parcels and passengers' luggage were conveyed and Mr Hooper
also arranged for post chaises and saddle horses. In short, the
techniques of the business were well known in the far west.

Interworking with other forms of transport came on the
scene at a fairly early date and we read in Battle's Hull directory for 1791 that

London coach sets out from Mr Thomas Walkers, Barton
Waterside every day (Saturday excepted) arrives at Lin-
coln the 1st day, Sleaford the 2nd day and at the Spread
Eagle in Gracechurch Street, London the 3rd day. Fare
inside £2 2s, outside £1 4s Mr Robert Dean, Agent,
Blackfriargate, Hull.

The important point is that passengers from Hull had to
cross the River Humber by ferry in order to join the coach.
As the ferries operated to an advertised timetable it was quite
practical to offer a co-ordinated facility that was much shorter
than the journey along the north bank to join one of the
coaches plying the Great North Road. By 1805 coach fares
had risen by over 50 per cent and an added innovation was
the use of carrier pigeons to despatch news to Hull inns on
the coach route. Spital-in-the-Street, Lincolnshire, a coaching
halt some thirty direct miles from Hull, had such an inn.
The news of the death of George III was delivered to Hull

by this means. Steamers sailed from the Humber to a number of foreign ports and there was much business for a variety of coach routes which operated both in connection with the deep sea and river services. On the adverse side the development of river services for passengers and cargo had the effect of putting some coaches out of business. By 1833 steamers from Hull connected at Gainsborough with coaches to Newark, Retford and Sheffield which interconnected with services on the Great North Road. The mail from London to Hull came by coach to Barton (later New Holland) from where it was conveyed across the Humber by ferry to Hull.

So at the end of the eighteenth century the pioneers of public transport for passengers and goods had established techniques and were poised on the threshold of the social and industrial revolution which had established itself in this country.

CHAPTER THREE

THE DRIVING FORCE

THE COACHMEN

STOUT, ROUGH, brutal men with red faces and hoarse voices—this is the popular view, and would be correct at any time between the introduction of coaches and 1820. No doubt there were thin men on the box camouflaged under the many layers of clothing, top boots and hats worn to keep out the cold. Their clothes encrusted by mud, whose livelihood was one of uncertainty, they little understood the art of coaching and were simply drivers; their task being as always to drive the horses and coach from inn to inn, using the whip to thrash the overworked horses to get the coach moving over the rough and ready tracks which passed for roads.

As coaching developed and the shorter stages replaced the day-long journeys, the standard of coachmen improved particularly with the introduction of the mail coaches culminating in the flower of the coaching age: coachmen who in the first quarter of the nineteenth century were always spotlessly clean with white beaver hats, box cloth coats, finishing their attire with neat cravats and a posy in their button holes. They were experts in dress and in management of their horses. Coaching became fashionable with those who today would be called the 'young men about town' and young men of the nobility were taught by the professionals to drive four-in-hand. As a result the two classes came together with the coachmen and the amateurs copying and exaggerating the most noticeable features of each other in dress, habit and speech. Those coachmen who took their dress to the extreme were known as 'flashmen', always dressing in the extreme of fashion and of whom it was said: 'Had a missus at both ends of the road, smoked a dozen real Havanahs in a hundred miles, and hardly thanked you for half a crown.' Men learned to handle horses and then coaches much as today people who drive cars graduate to bigger and more complex vehicles such as buses and articulated lorries. The best way to learn the art of driving was to get on the box seat and watch the coachman's hands.

Before horses could be driven satisfactorily they had to be properly put together, and to this end anyone who aspired to be a coachman needed a practical knowledge of how his team should be harnessed and 'put to the coach'. It has been truly remarked that horses which would pull together were half driven. The pole chains have not to be too slack because if the pace was fast, there was a tendency to make the coach rock. A team to go easily required a load proportioned to its power. There was much argument over the fitting of blinkers and it was reasoned by Cobbett in an *Old Coachman's Chatter*, that a horse from the position of his eye, had the power of seeing a long way behind him, which is necessary to him for his safety in a wild state, as he depends very largely for defence on his heels. Consequently any object which alarms him continues in sight for a long time. Therefore when in harness he felt blinkers to be essential.

A coachman before boarding would check the reins for free-running, settling them on the fingers of his left hand and would not let them out of his grasp whilst he mounted the box. Some horses would brook no delay and the coachman had to be ready for the off almost before he was seated. Accidents from failure to check could happen to the best coachmen and one evening after dark Charles Tustin, with the up Aberystwyth and Shrewsbury mail, as he was driving out of Newtown, found when he wanted to turn at the end of the first street, that the near wheel draught rein would not run, and consequently the coach came into collision with the corner shop. If Tustin had taken a pull at the reins as he usually did he would have found that the horsekeeper had carelessly fastened the rein in question between the hame and the collar. The coachman once on the box sat with his feet close together, arms hanging naturally. The reins would not be put down during a journey. So with the right hand holding the taut leads, the coachman's left hand was now free to take up the whip, which rested waiting on the wheelers' backs. He would mount passing the leads to his left hand, checking the tautness of the horses' traces again, signifying curtly to the ostler that he was ready to go, then, with a slight yielding of the rein-hand, let the horses pull. The coach was off. A contemporary postmaster describes the routine:

Two minutes ere the coach is due to start,
He casts a practised eye on every part,
Behind the wheel-horse, on the off-side stands,
Checking fulfillment of his nice demands,
Walks slowly round the back with comment blunt,
Comes to the rear-side, crossing then in front,
Looks at the leaders, sees the harness sits,
The reins correctly buckled to the bits,
Back on the off-side once again he stands,
Taking the reins, unlooped, in knowing hands,
First, in the left, drawing the lead-reins tight,
Against his hips, then passing to the right,

Which hand receives the wheel-reins too, to clap,
Each of the four within a finger grip.

The coachman had great stamina and skill which was best
demonstrated when he drove out of the inn-yard. Although
there was no greater test of a coachman's skill than the way he
took a heavy coach—sometimes weighing 3 tons or more—
down a steep hill. Early coaches had no brakes and halted at
the top of the hill for the guard to tie one of the rear wheels
with either the chain or skid-pan. Even so great strength was
needed by the two wheelers who if not strong enough to hold
back the coach on a hill might allow it to roll out of control,
slew round and turn over. Furthermore the coachman had to
ensure that the leaders did not draw the coach. Some of the
worst accidents occurred, when a coachman determined to
keep time was too impatient to stop at the top of every steep
hill to tie and untie a wheel. Even so a badly loaded coach
with a tied wheel and the slight skidding effect it produced
could easily turn over. Ascending steep hills was also a problem for the coachmen and it was common practice for passengers to have to get out and walk. The following passage, from
A Tale of Two Cities, refers to the Dover mail as it slowly
ascended Shooters Hill:

> He walked up hill in the mire by the side of the mail, as
> the rest of the passengers did; not because they had the
> least relish for walking exercise, under the circumstances,
> but because the hill, and the harness and the mud, and
> the mail, were all so heavy, that the horses had three times
> already come to a stop, besides once drawing the coach
> across the road, with the mutinous intent of taking it
> back to Blackheath. Reins and whip and coachman and
> guard, however, in combination, had read that article of
> war which forbad a purpose otherwise strongly in favour
> of the argument, that some brute animals are endowed
> with Reason; and the team capitulated and returned to
> their duty.

With drooping heads and tremulous tails, they mashed their way through the thick mud, floundering and stumbling between whiles, as if they were falling to pieces at the larger joints. As often as the driver rested them and brought them to a stand, with a wary 'Wo-ho! so-ho, then!' the near leader violently shook his head and everything on it—like an unusually emphatic horse, denying that the coach could be got up the hill....

Harper, in *Stage and Mail in Days of Yore*, describes very well the admiration that was given to coachmen:

The coachman was a master of an arduous craft; everyone looked up to him, dropping his reins at the stage, contemptuously leaving his horses to the ostler's care, he lolled about the yard like a lord, hands in pockets, recognized by gentry and urchins alike, throwing the small change of horsey lore and trade cant to be picked up and hoarded like sovereigns. Every ragamuffin that has a coat to his back thrusts his hands into his pockets, rolls in his gait, talks slang and is an embryo Coachey.

Many coachmen started as post boys and the career of Tom Holtby, the crack Yorkshire coachman who drove the York to London section of the Edinburgh mail, is of considerable interest. A tall man of distinguished appearance his confident recklessness earned him the nickname of 'Rash Tom'; born in 1791 he started working as a post boy at Easingwold and graduated to the box seat when he was twenty-nine, first on the Highflyer and finally on the celebrated Edinburgh Mail which had commenced on 16 October 1786. It continued to run until 1842 and on its last journey Lord Wenlock, an amateur coachman, sent his footman to the park gates to ask Tom Holtby if he would drive the mail through his estate, Escrick Park. In the park his lordship and Sir John Lister Kaye met this famous mail in order to accompany it on its last

journey. Hoisting a huge black flag from the coach roof Lord
Macdonald took the ribbons and with Holtby sitting beside
him they terminated the last journey at the Black Swan, York.
'Remember the coachman, sir,' said Lord Macdonald, slyly
touching his hat and nudging Tom with his elbow. 'So I will,'
answered Tom, 'if your lordship will likewise remember the
guard.' 'Well I'll give him double what you give me, anyhow.'
'Done,' said Tom, as he whipped a fiver into Lord Macdonald's hand. As his lordship handed £10 to the guard, Tom
Day, he remarked, 'I have had you for £5 anyhow Tom.' 'Not
a bit of it, my lord; Day and I understand each other; I shall
clear £2 10s by the transaction.'

With the cessation of coaching Tom Holtby, a constant
attendant at York races, became involved in several unsuccessful financial ventures, but when he died on 1 June 1863 aged
seventy-two years he was worth £3,000.

John Frederic Herring was a natural artist who, with his
young wife, arrived penniless in Doncaster in 1814. Commencing as a signwriter and illustrator on stage coach bodies
he soon became coachman on the Highflyer and divided his
time between driving coaches and painting inn signs. It was,
however, as a painter of race horses that he achieved his fame,
and giving up the ribbons in 1821 he rose to become painter
to the queen.

There was a sharp distinction between London and provincial coachmen and Yorkshire bye roads were regarded with
contempt in coaching circles both for their coaches and coachmen. One reads of dirty coaches in Yorkshire in 1830 drawn
by a team of 'like' horses known as Rumbleguts, Bumblekite,
Staggering Bob and Davey. On the cross roads the coachmen
changed with every stage and cleaned and harnessed their
own horses. In the remote parts they were a hundred years
behind the advanced methods of coaching practised in other
parts of the country.

The age of coachmen varied but in 1837 Harry Ward, who

drove the Quicksilver from Andover to Salisbury, was twenty-
four and to his last day was proud of the fact that he had never
had an accident on any road although once in reply to the
question of a passenger said, 'This is the twentieth brandy
and water today but you soon get it blown out of you crossing
Salisbury Plain.' It was not so easy a matter to make a seasoned
coachman drunk.

Tipping originated with the first stage coach journey and
the amounts expected by the coachman developed over the
years and was related to the smartness of the coach and the
class of passengers conveyed, especially the amateurs who
would give the coachman a guinea or half a guinea.

In the Golden Age the amateur coachman (who was a
product of the nineteenth century) resulted in the art of
galloping teams becoming a fashionable amusement. It first
arose on the Brighton road in the early nineteenth century
and the education of no gay young blood was complete until
he had acquired the art of four-in-hand driving. A 'real gentleman' was one who flung away his money in tips and many
'young oxonians' or 'young cantabs', with more taste for driving four-in-hand than knowledge of art, were frequent aspir-
ants for the ribbons. Not unnaturally professional coachmen
on the Oxford and Cambridge roads made plenty of hard cash
out of this enthusiasm, but the passengers saw it very differ-
ently, galloping at the incredible speed of 20mph, the coach
rocking violently, while the outsides held on like frightened
men, and the insides prayed for a safe arrival. Coach proprietors dreaded the amateurs and instantly dismissed any
coachman in their employ who allowed one to drive. Accidents
were fairly numerous in any case and the likelihood was much
higher if the professional was not holding the ribbons, and in
settlement of compensation claims, juries assessed damages in
relation to whether the professional or the amateur was driving. The Brighton road was very popular with the amateurs
amongst whom were the Marquis of Worcester who ran the

Wonder and the Honourable Fred Jerningham who drove the
day mail. Perhaps the most famous was Sir St Vincent Cotton
who was the cause of a serious accident to the Star of Cambridge which he drove at such a reckless pace that the coach
overturned. The injuries to passengers were such that Robert
Nelson and his partners had to pay out nearly £2,000. Having
dissipated his fortune, he ran his own coach, the Age, which
he had taken over on the death of its founder Harry Steven-
son. Passengers travelling on the Age were refreshed at intervals by a liveried servant with a glass of sherry and sandwiches
on a silver plate.

It was said of the amateur coachman (and no doubt any
coachman) that

> He who would master this most fascinating science of
> coachmanship must begin early, under good tuition. He
> must work constantly on all forms of coaches and thereby
> accustoming himself to every description of team to be
> met with, no matter how difficult or unpleasant, will he
> acquire a practical knowledge on that all important point,
> the art of putting horses well together.

A large number of clubs were formed, such as the Four in
Hand, which had considerable influence in the development
of the art of driving and coach design.

The most trying time for the coachmen and guards was the
first two hours on the road at night. After that, few vehicles
were moving about, but up to that time a large number, many
unlighted, were in motion. Both had to keep a sharp look out
and on foggy nights the guard made frequent use of his horn
to warn of the coach's presence.

Not all the travellers supported the fast coaches where competition was greater and many preferred the slower ones,
whose proprietors discovered to their pleasure that there was
a profitable business to be made from the timid. Coach pro-

Page 53 'Behind Time.' The Highflyer and Comet passing on the Leeds–York road

Page 54 (above) The Liverpool–London Royal Mail which commenced running on 1 January 1836; (below) Royal Telegraph Manchester–London day coach which covered the distance of 186 miles in eighteen hours in 1833

prietors were well aware of the subtleties of their business and, as Charles Dickens wrote, 'Coaches, Sammy, is like guns —they requires to be loaded with very great care, afore they go off.'

The original purpose of stage coach guards was to guard the coaches against attack, but gradually they came to look after way bills and passengers' luggage until some proprietors discontinued guards on the fast day coaches where prospect of attack was remote. This led in the latter years of coaching to several accidents directly attributed to the coachman leaving his coach and horses unattended. The original guards were versatile men, in many cases, capable of taking over the ribbons; some were cheerful loquacious men like George Young, guard of the Leeds Union, who met his death as a result of sitting in an unsafe place, because he gave his seat to an extra passenger. Bob Hadley of the Union coach between Manchester and the Potteries was noted for his eccentric clothing and headgear. One of the duties of the guard was to blow his coach horn, the old yard of tin, to warn of the coach's approach and this extended in the last twenty years of coaching to the guard's musical accomplishment on the key bugle imported from Germany in 1818. Favourite tunes were *Cherry Ripe*, the *Huntsman's Chorus*, *Sally in our Alley* and other pop tunes of the age. No doubt there were good and bad players, the latter being unlikely to enrich a long journey. The Post Office forbade the mail guards to play key bugles and whilst they complied in the London area they utilised their forbidden instruments to the full in the country. A famous provincial coach was the Rockingham which ran between Leeds and London from 1787 until 1844. One of its famous guards was William Motrham who liked to quote the incident of the Irishman and Chesterfield Church. Motrham told a good story explaining why the spire was not perpendicular and went on to give a detailed account as to how it was to be straightened on the very next day. 'Begorry, thin, Oi'll just stip and see it

D

done,' and complete with luggage the Irishman was set down
at the roadside. History, unfortunately, does not record his
views of humorous coach guards. It was the guard who
checked the tickets, supervised passengers and their luggage,
recorded times of arrival and departure, inspected the wheels
and axles of the vehicle, and paid turnpike dues. It seems
there were exceptions in the allocation of duties as Cobbett
writes in an *Old Coachman's Chatter*:

When I was driving the Snowdonian upon one up journey, upon looking at the way bill, as I left Dolgelly, I
perceived that there was a lady booked, to be taken up a
mile or two out of town to go a short distance, the fare for
which was 3s 6d 'to pay'. She took her place in the coach
in due course, and having alighted at her destination, I
demanded her fare from her, upon which she assured me
she could only pay 2s 6d as she had no more money with
her. I told her I was responsible for the full fare, and that
she really must pay it; and when she saw that I was determined to have no nonsense about it, she asked me if I
could give her change for a sovereign, to which I replied,
'Yes, or two, if you like'; whereupon, she opened her
purse and exposed to my delighted eyes two or three
shiners.

Charles Dickens describes very well the departures of a
coach and the associated duties of the coachman and guards:

But the guard has delivered at the corn-dealer's shop the
brown paper packet he took out of the little pouch which
hangs over his shoulder by a leathern strap; and has seen
the horses carefully put to; and has thrown onto the pavement the saddle which was brought from London on the
coach-roof; and has assisted in the conference between
the coachman and the hostler about the grey mare that
hurt her off foreleg last Tuesday; and he and Mr Weller

are all right behind, and the coachman is all right in
front and the old gentleman inside who has kept the
window down full two inches all this time, has pulled it
up again, and the cloths are off, and they are all ready for
starting, except the 'two stout gentlemen', whom the
coachman inquires after with some impatience. Here-
upon the coachman, and the guard, and Sam Weller, and
Mr Winkle, and Mr Snodgrass, and all the hostlers, and
every one of the idlers, who are more in number than all
the others put together, shout for the missing gentleman
as loud as they can. A distant response is heard from the
yard and Mr Pickwick and Mr Tupman come running
down it, quite out of breath, for they have been having a
glass of ale a piece, and Mr Pickwick's fingers are so cold
that he has full five minutes before he could find the six-
pence to pay for it. The coachman shouts an admonitory
'Now then gen'l'm'n!'; the guard re-echoes it; the old
gentleman inside thinks it a very extraordinary thing
that people will get down when they know there isn't
time for it; Mr Pickwick struggles up on one side, Mr
Tupman on the other; Mr Winkle cries 'All right'; and
off they start. Shawls are pulled up, coat collars are re-
adjusted, the pavement ceases, the houses disappear, and
they once again go dashing along the open road, with the
fresh clear air blowing in their faces, and gladdening
their very hearts within them.

It was the Golden Age chiefly from the sportsman's point of
view in the projection of coach building and harness making,
the smartness of the horses, and the speeds attained. At this
time a few proprietors made fortunes but many ended in
bankruptcy court. The biggest increase in costs related to
provision of horses which had to be replaced every three years
due to exertions on the fast coaches. They were generally
purchased by farmers and traders and lived out their lives in
comfort whilst their more unfortunate brothers hauled the
coaches. The stages were out and home 6 or 7 miles as opposed

to the 10 or 11 miles single journey. Many coachmen objected to two sweats a day but they had the advantage that the horses were cared for in their own stables. The fastest schedules now required one horse for every route mile for each coach on the roads. Supply and care of the horses was a business similar to that of the motor trade today, but the livery and other stables were more common than commercial garages. Second-hand animals were offered for sale like second-hand cars and were sold through repositories and dealers, and through newspaper and other advertisements. Horses that gave trouble to their owners—biters, jibbers, kickers and roamers, for example— were offered to the coach proprietors since it was thought that in this less refined work their vices did not matter. The cost of buying varied enormously and averaged in 1833 between £23 and £37 depending upon the particular auction, although some horses at these auctions sold for much higher prices with £100 being the price paid for a brown gelding. Another indication is given in a newspaper report of 14 June 1817: 'A few days ago Mr Webb, a coach proprietor of Lichfield, lost two valuable horses, worth 100 guineas almost at the same instant, both being killed by loose stones on the road.' Provided a horse was sound in wind and limb, any vicious habits were soon disciplined hauling the coaches, with the result that some of doubtful origin were purchased very cheap. The coachman's ideal was a matching team in stride but this was unimportant to the coach proprietor and where such teams existed they were usually employed on the stages into or out of London. The number of horses that had to be used on a particular run depended very much on the state of the roads. Contractors were not always diligent in this respect and the Post Office found it necessary to point out the failures of certain of their number to have their horses' shoes prepared for winter travelling.

The Post Office is dissatisfied with many of the contractors and their servants, who when they must have known the necessity neglected to have their horses' shoes prepared for the frost and slippery road, by which time has been lost. It is hoped that contractors will now be careful for their own sakes, as well as from a sense of duty, to have the shoes roughed, and save their horses from falling and injuring themselves and creating delays.

The Post Office was very jealous of its record of punctuality for which it had a great need to properly operate the system of connections.

Training horses was (and is) a skilled profession and we were very fortunate in being given a practical demonstration by Iain Macauley (of Charlecote Carriages, Charlecote, Warwick) who is an authority on breaking in horses for four-in-hand teams and indeed any other horses required to pull a cart or carriage. He uses the old methods and a breaking-in cart dating from 1900. The horse is first fitted with the various pieces of harness for a number of days until the animal is quite used to the feel of them. The horses usually average about five years old and have been ridden. Each horse is then separately introduced to the breaking-in cart, which is an ordinary cart with extension shafts. For the first two trips in the cart a breast collar is used, then an open collar. After each horse is used to pulling a cart, two horses are put together in a normal carriage, then the full team of four, so the full team is slowly introduced and taught to work together. For the first few trips in the breaking-in cart a groom is used to hold the horse's head in case of any nervous bucking. The horses best suited for team work are ones with a good shoulder and a big open foot and having a quiet temperament. Iain Macauley said that in his experience geldings were more easily trained than mares. He told us that a trick used years ago by the trainers of coach horses that had the fault of over pulling, was to tether them to a tree upon which they were encouraged to pull until they eventually tired of the habit and ran without straining and putting the other horses out of balance.

The two leaders and wheelers made up the team known as 'cattle'. Horses were used so brutally that three years was their maximum working life, although in later years four years on the fast coaches and seven on the slow coaches became more usual. The term 'to die in harness' comes from these times and it was true, for in 1821 twenty horses dropped dead on one mail coach route alone. Care was taken to ensure the horses looked well, particularly on the day coaches, but diseases abounded and ill horses were put onto the night runs when the horror could not be seen. 'Hit them as can work,' counselled one veteran. 'It's no use hitting them as can't.' The coachman's objective was to run on time, and he used his whip to achieve this—the horses meant nothing to him. The RSPCA was founded in 1824 but coachmen had never heard of it or bothered about it. On the London–Edinburgh run well over a hundred charges were made. Galloping did not generally take place as the horses could move the coach at 10mph at a fast trot, for a 10-mile stage, but to increase the speed to 13mph, with considerable risk to horses, passengers and coach, was not worth the trouble when it could not be maintained for much over 4 miles.

The hazards of night travel sprang from the dishonesty of the contractors who horsed the night coaches with unsound or vicious horses which they dare not show in daylight. Similarly at night they could get away with harness that was too old to be safe and coachmen, too, were more likely to be drunk, although to overcome this the coachmen regularly tipped the horse keepers to secure their goodwill.

But when all is said and done it was the coachman and guard who made the coach service function. Many gave their lives through accident and some through duty. Two such men were James MacGeorge and John Goodfellow who died

near Moffat in February 1831 when they set out walking together through snow drifts which were impassable for coach
or saddle horse. On the following day the mail bags were
found lashed to a post near the roadside but it was not until
several days afterwards that their bodies were dug out of the
snow. Indeed they were the 'driving force' in maintaining
the tradition that the post must get through.

CHAPTER FOUR

STAGE COACHES IN THE GOLDEN AGE

IT WAS about 1800 that front and rear boots became general and with suitable foothold and seat gave a safer journey for the outsiders. The result was to democratise coach travel; exclusive insides were 'obliged to suffer a set of cheap travellers, who were always to be found on the roof, laughing and talking loudly, enjoying themselves in the elementary and vociferous style only possible to low persons, and disturbing the genteel reflections of the insides'.

Returning to the theme of naming coaches to attract traffic was the endeavour to contact all categories of traveller. Regular or Reliance for the cautious, but Lightening, Highflyer or Spitfire for the sportsman; coaches were also named after great victories and heroes: so we have in 1805 Nelsons, Lord Nelsons and Trafalgars. Class distinction and snobbery led to a need for a coach carrying 'insiders only'; for instance the nautically termed Land Frigate which was

A New carriage on springs and sets out from the Bell Savage, Ludgate Hill, to the Red Lyon at Portsmouth, every Tuesday and Saturday at 6am. Fare 15s each passenger. Ladies and Gentlemen are requested to observe that the Frigate is elegantly sashed all round, and in order to preserve the gentility and respectability of the vehicle no outside passengers are carried.

Etiquette was such that no passenger without a hat was allowed to ride in or on a stage coach.

The first decade of the nineteenth century saw two of the most significant advances in the history of coaching: first the institution, about 1805, of springs under the driving box seat (due to the suggestion of John Warde, earliest of the coaching amateurs) which enabled coachmen to drive greater distances; and second, the shortening of the stages. From the early days when a team of horses remained with the same coach from origin to destination there came a reduction to 20-mile stages and then to 10-mile stages with change of coachmen at intervals so that continuous running could be achieved. These factors combined with improvements in the roads and the example of the mails which had largely brought this about saw the coaches now adhering to their published timetables. They now started instead of setting out, the term 'God permits' no longer appeared and the coaches arrived 'God willing or not'. The acceleration in speeds which resulted in the Golden Age of coaching beginning in 1825 had been made possible by the improvements of the roads. Coaches displayed many destinations other than they served and this in itself was an indication of the reliability achieved which permitted through indirect journeys by interchange of passengers at intermediate places on route.

Stage coach conversation for the insides in the days before the fast coaches was an art and a man who discussed politics

Daily Direct & Cheap Conveyance.

THE
Perseverance
COACH,
From Grimsby to Louth, Horncastle, and Boston
To LONDON.

THE COACH SETS OUT FROM THE
Mary Tavern, Grimsby,
Every Day on the Landing of the Hull Packets.

FARES:

	INSIDE.		OUTSIDE.	
	£. s. d.		£. s. d.	
From Grimsby to Louth	0 1 0		NOTHING	
From Grimsby to Horncastle	0 6 0		0 3 0	
From Grimsby to Boston	0 12 0		0 6 0	

N.B. Passengers Booked by W. SENIOR, the LONDON TAVERN direct for *London*, for £1 5s. Outside, £2 6s. Inside.

For Particulars inquire at W. SENIOR's, LONDON TAVERN, HULL.

TOPPING and DAWSON, Printers, 47, Lowgate, Hull.

Fig 2 Advertisement for Grimsby–London (Perseverance) stage coach

before the coach was clear of the outskirts of London was thought too excessively forward and talkative. Considerable small talk with great discretion was the rule until you had an opportunity to size up your companions. The best opening conversational gambit was, 'Well we are now off the stones. What a beautiful morning! How charming the outskirts of town! Pray, does not that house belong to ——?' It was the custom to walk up the hills and, heaven forbid, one was allowed on these occasions to talk with the outsiders provided they understood that such familiarity would not be resumed at the inn! But not so with the fast coaches travelling at 11mph—for one thing the noise drowned out conversation, timekeeping was sacred and, as Hine a coach proprietor on the Brighton road said in 1831, 'Lord Sir, we don't travel half so uncomfortably now as we used to do. It is all hurry and bustle nowadays sir—no time even for a pipe and a glass of grog.'

Cobbett wrote about the spectacle of a coach coming in, when the horses were all sweat and foam, the reek from their bodies ascending like a cloud. The whole equipage was covered with dust and dirt. But still it came on as steady as the hand of the clock. As a proof of the perfection to which this mode of travelling had been brought, there was one coach which ran between Exeter and London whose proprietors agreed to forfeit 8d for every minute the coach was behind its time at any of its stages. Another famous coach of the time was the Tantivy which commenced in 1832 on a route between London and Birmingham via Maidenhead, Henley, Oxford, Woodstock, Shipton-on-Stour and Stratford-on-Avon —a distance of 125 miles in twelve hours dead. Departing at 7am from London it averaged 11mph and was once driven through its journey in a single sitting by Cracknell, the most famous coachman on the Tantivy. The naming of coaches in this competitive business continued to be the source of much inspiration and Telegraph was very popular with the Telegraph and New Telegraph on the Brighton road, and to compete with the Quicksilver Mail the Exeter Telegraph was introduced to run the 173 miles in seventeen hours, which was later reduced by three hours before the coach was driven off the road by the Great Western Railway.

In the way of the modern motor-coach with its driver-conductor it is interesting to note that the Brighton Comet running from 1815 to 1840 was manned solely by the coachman, who also carried out the duties of the guard. Coaches were often renamed to suit the mood of the moment with a view to attracting passengers from the supposedly less astute competitors. All the aggressiveness, dash, competition and sparkle of the Golden Age was contained in the name emblazoned on the coaches—there were Rapids, Expresses, Retaliators, Dreadnaught, Invincible, and at the other end of the scale Live and Let Live, Hope, Endeavour and Perseverance amongst many others. For the reassurance of the timid we find the so-called Patent Safeties which in many cases were neither Patent nor Safe but a Retaliator in another guise. However, public concern at the ever growing number of accidents brought forward various inventions and in 1819 a new design of coach took the road. Called the Sovereign it was larger but lighter than the general stage coach, had smaller wheels and the passengers' accommodation was relocated so that the outsides were seated in a landau with the closed parts of the body at the rear. Several similar vehicles were built but they did not come into general use.

A north country coach—the Hero—put on the road in 1832 is of particular interest, named after a champion fighting cock in the North of England. This coach was started by the proprietors of *The Times* and the *Telegraph* who introduced it as a night coach between Leeds and Newcastle to connect there for Edinburgh. Their objective was to run the North Courier, which operated over the same route, off the road. The route was via Harrogate, Knaresborough, Boroughbridge, North Allerton, Darlington and Durham. Despite racing and fare cutting the scheme did not succeed as both coaches continued to run for many years, being joined by the Red Rover which operated via Leeming and Catterick. Probably a typical scheme of the times, the coach is unusual in that it was rebuilt in 1970 by George Darley of Ganstead in Yorkshire. Abandoned in a field at the end of the coaching days it was left to rot until just over a hundred years later it was dragged from its resting place and taken to Mr Darley's joinery establishment. In its prime the coach was painted dark green and primrose, with a magnificent illustration of the fighting cock displayed on the doors.

In the restoration three of the wheels were rebuilt by Mr Darley using techniques handed down from father to son. Other parts recovered included most of the ironwork but the woodwork (such as remained) was unusable. The construction of the new body was accomplished with only the aid of a general outline drawing and the opportunity to inspect other coaches in local collections. Originally coach bodies were constructed from ash for the framing and $\frac{1}{2}$in mahogany for the panels. Although patterns were used by the other builders each firm had tricks of their own, which were jealously guarded. In general the panels were covered on the inside with white lead onto which was laid hessian. This was painted with two coats of thick paint into which the hessian was worked. When dry a final coat of paint was applied and the resultant effect was a strong panel without the tendency to split. Ash was used in the restoration of the Hero but plywood was used for the panels; otherwise the practices of the old coachbuilders were followed—not from books but from inherited knowledge. The cost of building the new coach was about £1,000 for 536 hours work in construction, to which must be added the painting and provision of harness. Eleven coats of paint and three of varnish were used, after priming. To compensate for the variations in weights

when running loaded or unloaded, the wheels were angled
inwards from the centre about ⅜in and for forward drag angled
in a similar distance to the body. When the coach is running
the wheels run square and in a vertical plane. If the coach
was not running properly because it was out of true, coachmen
could compensate by adjusting the traces so that the horse
behind pulled to catch the others up, thereby correcting the
running. Coach horses were generally a foot shorter in the
body than draught horses. The pole linking the axles was
called the spring pole in the North of England but the
perch in the South. There were probably other names and
it occurred in many cases that similar parts had different
names. It is particularly interesting to compare Mr Darley's
restoration with the Post Office's requirements for mail coach
construction. The following is an extract from John Copeland's *Roads and their Traffic 1750–1850*:

A detailed specification of the mail coaches is given in a
Post Office statement of 1839. The extreme length of the
coach measured from the bottom of the foot board to the
end of the mail box, was 10ft 8in, and the extreme height
exactly over the door was 7ft 2in. The distance between
the fore and hind axles was 6ft 6in and the width of the
track from the outside of the felloes, was 5ft 1½in. The
fore wheels were given as 42in diameter and the rear
wheels as 54in, the width of the rounded tyre being 1⅞in.
Materials were specified as follows:
Body—Parts covered with leather. Deal panels and floor
    mahogany. Fore boot frame—ash; fit deal case covered
    with leather.
Mail box—Frame ash. Fit casing covered with leather.
Pole—Ash, Pole hook and chains, with swivel collar and
    fastenings. Drag shoe and chain.
Under carriage—Ash.
Felloes—Beech or Ash.
Spokes—Oak, stock elm.
Bars—Ash.

Inside the coach was drab lace lining with double crimson stripes, with a carpet to match. Mahogany glass frames, with only one square of glass in each, were fitted; and the cushions were stuffed with the best horsehair. Oilcloth was fitted to the bottom of the coach, and there were two pockets on each door. Interior measurements given included 18½in legroom, a height from the top of the seat of 42½in and a width of 43½in.

Concurrent with the improvement in roads there had been improvements in the quality of horses and staff who ran the coaches, which themselves had been improved in the building, upholstery and general appearance. Competition which had forced the pace on the road now led to rate cutting with fares tumbling until it was possible to travel from London to Birmingham for £1 inside and 10s outside and to Manchester and Liverpool for £2 inside and £1 outside—less than half the 1833 rates. The forerunner of the horsebus was the short stage coaches which, drawn by a pair of horses, operated several journeys daily to the suburbs of London from inns and coach offices in the city and the West End. Incredibly large numbers of these vehicles were gradually replaced after 1829 by the omnibus developed from Shillibeer's project of 1829. Monsieur L. Simond described in extremely critical terms a journey in a short stage coach between Richmond and London at the beginning of 1810. He said that the coach was:

crammed inside and outside with passengers, of all sexes, ages and conditions. We stopped more than twenty times on the road the debates about the fare of way-passengers—the settling themselves the getting up, and the getting down—and the damsels shewing their legs in the operation and tearing and mudding their petticoats—complaining and swearing—took an immense time. I never saw anything so ill-managed. In about two hours we reached Hyde Park corner...

These short-distance stage coaches, however, performed a valuable service.

In the second decade of the nineteenth century Glasgow was expanding but there was little travelling by its inhabitants. This was soon to change and by 1825 there were ten daily coaches to Edinburgh alone. Glasgow was one of the first cities in Britain to establish regulations for coachmen, street porters and inn yard staff:

> Not more than six porters shall resort to, or take up station at, any Coach Office, Inn or other place at which Stage Coaches arrive. On the arrival of Coaches, the porters shall stand in a line on the kirb-stone of the pavement; and they shall not leave the kirb-stone, or interfere with passengers' luggage, until singled out and engaged. They shall not importune, call out or make any signal to passengers for employment; and, unless specially selected by passengers, they shall take turn in rotation, each in regular succession... No porter shall appear on his station intoxicated; if he does, he shall be removed, and the next in order shall take his place. All porters are prohibited from standing on the pavement or crossings, to the obstruction or annoyance of the lieges; as also from smoking when upon their stations, or in any manner giving offence.

For porterage a maximum charge was established of 2d a quarter mile with a light load and 3d with a heavy one. Despite the regulations the porter's job was much sought after; it carried rank, and with rank went respect. In Scotland there were several experiments with large coaches. The Royal Oak which ran to Greenock was a double decker drawn by six horses and accommodating forty passengers, whereas The Royal Caledonian Basket could convey twenty-six. It was a

Page 71 (above) Mail coach in the snow; note the postilion on the near leader with the extra pair of horses; (below) stage coach travelling (painted by J. Pollard)

Page 72 (above) North country mails at the Peacock, Islington; *(below)* the post boy at a turnpike gate, c1830

mail coach, draped in a black flag, which entered Paisley on a night in October 1831 amid a near rioting mob, to bring the news that the Scottish Reform Bill had been defeated in the House of Lords.

In 1825 there was a project to light the interior of coaches with gas and in January 1827 coaches so equipped were tried, unsuccessfully we must record, between Glasgow and Paisley bringing forth the comment from an old woman, 'Guid lord Sandy, they've laid gas pipes all the way from Glasgow Cross to Paisley.'

In the 1830s Glasgow competed with Edinburgh and Aberdeen for the honour of being Scotland's principal coaching centre. The coaching offices were, in common with other cities, scattered around the city. The great mail coach office, booking passengers to Edinburgh and London and all parts of the country, consisted of a small room in the lower department of one of the tenements in Nelson Street, and a pie and porter shop stood nearby, on the corner of it. The pealing of church bells from the Tron steeple fifteen minutes before the departure time of the night mail to England was a unique feature of the Glasgow coaching scene. Of twenty-four mail coaches which ran in Scotland, nine worked out of the city, departing from 64 Trongate, two each day to Edinburgh and one to Perth, Stirling, Aberdeen, Carlisle, Leeds, London and Portpatrick. Many of the stage coaches also ran from Trongate, those to Paisley, Greenock and Renfrew from number 78; three of the twenty-four daily coaches to Edinburgh as well as the Earl of Mar to Alloa and Tillicoultry departed from number 100, the latter coach terminating at the picturesquely named Clackmannanshire inn, The Pay the Day and Trust the Morn. From Argyle Street, coaches ran to destinations south of the border: to Edinburgh, Carlisle and Stirling and the Royal Bruce to London. Other coaches departed from inns around Gallowgate and High Street, and Cobbett pictures their departure for us:

E

Next to a fox-hunt the finest sight in England is a stage coach just ready to start. A great sheep or cattle fair is a beautiful sight; but in a stage coach you see more of what man is capable of performing. The vehicle itself; the harness, all so complete and neatly arranged, so strong and clean and good; the beautiful horses, impatient to be off; the inside full and the outside covered, in every part, with men, women and children, boxes, bags, bundles; the coachman, taking his reins in one hand and the whip in the other, gives a signal with his foot and away they go, at a rate of seven miles an hour.

Travel in the north of Scotland during the winter was an ordeal, so much so that it was very rare for women to travel as outsides. Ordinary coats and hats gave little protection against the weather and the travelling rug and the Inverness cape (the first item of clothing specifically for coach travel) did not come onto the scene until thousands of passengers had endured countless hours of misery. As one contemporary writer records, the 'futile umbrella was still in ordinary use. The rain beat down your neck; the sleet was driven in at every button hole; your overcoat was speedily saturated'. He further wrote:

I have fought frost and bitter North Sea breezes myself, when sitting crumpled up and crouching behind the coachman's back on the roof of the Royal Mail or Defiance. Serious smashes were rare, but drowsiness difficult to guard against. The outsiders on the seats behind the coach-box or facing the guard were hanging between heaven and earth. One foot was on the slippery straw on the foot-board, the other often dangling in space. Even when wide awake, a lurch might prove awkward; and there were sharp corners in the narrow streets of many an antiquated burgh town, where the top-heavy vehicle took a perilous swing. When you began to nod toward nightfall, or dropped into a snooze in the small hours, you were sitting in the very shadow of Death.

On the box you were somewhat safer, for you were under the eye of a very experienced coachman.

In later days when going north for salmon-fishing or grouse-shooting, I used to catch at Inverness the northern mail for Tain or Dingwall. One glorious spring morning I scrambled up beside the driver, an old acquaintance. Had I refreshed myself with laudanum instead of rum and milk I could not have felt more sleepy. It is a grand bit of galloping ground that skirts the Firth, and my friend put his horses along. The ocean ozone, laden with the intoxicating fragrance of the sea-wrack might have lulled a victim of chronic insomnia, and if the driver's elbow had not been kept continually in my ribs I should certainly have been a subject for the coroner's inquest, had there been such things to the north of the Tweed.

It was not only in winter that travelling was tiring but in summer also. One can try and imagine one traveller's spirits rising as in 1830 the London to Newcastle-on-Tyne coach nears its journey's end:

Changing at the Three Tuns (Durham) the new team toils painfully up the atrociously steep streets to Framwellgate Bridge, where the river Wear and the stone grandeur of the Norman Cathedral with the bold cocks and soft woods around it, blend under the westening sun-rays of a July evening into a lovely mellowed picture.

Chester-le-Street and Gateshead are ill-exchanges for the picturesqueness of Durham, but they serve to bring us nearer our journey's end, and truth to tell, we are very weary: so that coming down the break neck streets of Gateshead in the gathering darkness to the coaly Tyne and dear dirty Newcastle with the hum of its great population and the hooting of its steamers in our ears, we are filled with a great content. 'Give 'em a tune', says the coachman; and the guard sounding a fanfare, we are quickly over the old town bridge, along the Side and at the Turf Hotel, Collingwood Street, it is nearly 10 o'clock. The journey is done.

Punctuality was of utmost importance with certain runs scheduled to the half minute and careful allocation of departure times from London, which was very necessary when it is appreciated that in 1820, 1,500 coaches departed London every twenty-four hours. So good was timekeeping that a saying arose 'as right as the mails'. The stage coach was all urgency, and the guard's time piece, not the passengers', was king. The coaching era represents the beginning of modernity. In coaching parlance the streets of a town were called 'the stones' and 'the stones end' was where they gave way to the unmetalled surfaces of rural roads.

You hear the guard's horn, warning the next stage. Soon you come to the Blue Boar, but there is no alighting, except for the guard and whip. Fifty seconds is enough for each to down a watery glass, hot but not too hot. The change is waiting. Four horses are led off to the stables, all of a sweat; the four new ones are fitted in, neat as machinery. Aye, boy, Right boy, Guard and driver remount. The horn, the easing of the reins, off again.

An interesting service was operated by Messageries Royales of Paris from The White Bear, Piccadilly, London, to Dover, Calais and Paris. Passengers were conveyed by packet boat from Dover to Calais.

Coaches had more outside than inside accommodation and the following figures make interesting reading if related to actual loading and distribution of passengers (see Table).

COACH LEGISLATION

The legislators were early on the scene, first in the sphere of traffic regulations for highways, and by an Act of 1622

used for any specific purpose at any specific time. The laws were in fact framed to protect the road against the traders and an interesting point in the General Turnpike Act of 1766 (and other Acts) especially forbade waggoners to sit in, or drive from, their waggons. They had to either walk or ride beside them.

In 1776 a stamp office duty of £5 per annum was levied on stage coaches, added to in 1783 by a duty of $\frac{1}{2}$d per mile run, which in 1785 was amended to a 5s licence fee and a duty of 1d a mile. Seven days' notice was required of any coach being delicensed. Coaches were given a numbered licence, which had to be displayed. By Act of 1788 stage coaches were not permitted to carry more than six passengers on the roof or more than two on the box in addition to the coachman. For each additional passenger the coachman was liable to a fine of £2 and if proprietor or proprietors then this was increased to £4. This was subsequently amended so as to provide for coaches drawn by three or more horses to carry only one on the box and not more than four on the roof. Pair-horse coaches could only convey one on the box and three on the roof, except that if they were travelling in a 25-mile radius of London they might carry an additional passenger on the box. The penalty for infringement was 5s to be paid at each turnpike gate which ensured that detectives as well as the pike men would share in any fine. For fraudulently setting down a passenger before a gate and picking him up on the other side with intent to avoid this regulation the penalty was a term of imprisonment not less than fourteen days and not more than six months. The names of the proprietors had to be painted in legible letters on the doors of all stage coaches, but not on mail coaches. Further regulations under the Acts of 1788 and 1790 provided penalties for the coachman permitting other persons to drive, but the practice was not stopped by the Acts or the penalty. No coachman was to leave his box without reasonable cause or occasion, and furious driving was

legislated against as was negligence and misconduct leading
to a coach being overturned or passengers endangered.

> It is terrible, and none will do ought to stop it. Three
> killed last year, and two this year and the year not yet
> over. Death on the roads. Grown men racing each other
> like boys. They were right to clap those two in irons and
> give them hard labour for a year. Nay, they should have
> deported them to the colonies.

An Act of 1806 further revised the number of outsides and
specified their positions but this was again modified in 1811
(by an Act). A curious section which underlined the social
difference between insides and outsides provided that no
outside passenger could go inside the coach or remain inside
without consent of at least one inside next to whom the outside had then to sit. No luggage or person was permitted on
the roof of a coach if it caused it to be more than 10ft 9in
above the ground, and there were regulations for a height of
luggage, inspection and measurements were made by the
turnpike keeper and of course there were fines for infringement. Beware the passenger who sat on his luggage, or the
place reserved for it, for it could have cost him a fine of
£2 10s! Guards were forbidden to discharge their blunderbusses other than for defensive purposes. Intoxicated, insult-
ing, cheating coachmen, or those who drove dangerously,
could be fined or imprisoned and mail coach drivers, besides
having the distinction of automatically receiving the higher
penalties, could be penalised for loitering, or hindering the
conduct of His Majesty's mails to the next stage. The licence
regulations were further extended to provide for the precise
number of inside and outside passengers a coach could convey, running without a licence; carrying excess passengers
could count for a heavy fine and in certain cases imprisonment.

In practice passengers sat on their luggage if they felt so inclined, coachmen got drunk, drove furiously or allowed the deadly amateur to drive; luggage was stacked to alpine heights; guards discharged their blunderbusses everywhere from sheer wantonness or on joyful occasions, passengers were carried to excess; and indeed every provision of every Act was flagrantly violated, generally of malice aforethought, but in many instances from ignorance and the inability of coach proprietors and the others concerned to keep themselves fully informed on all points. The waggoners and even pikemen, the sworn enemies of all on the roads, both had great difficulty in complying with the regulations and became liable to penalties. It was forbidden that all four horses be permitted to gallop at the same time!

All these regulations served to further the activities of the professional informer by reason of the provision whereby the informer received the whole or share of the penalty upon conviction at the discretion of the magistrates. The roads swarmed with informers, some working singly, others constituted into firms. It is suggested that on some routes coach proprietors and waggoners were alleged to make annual payments to informers to dissuade them from laying information, which might result in a prosecution:

To James Cheriston of Kingston Stage Coach proprietor. Whereas complaint and Information hath been made upon oath before me Sir John Pinkhorn one of his Majesty's Justices of the Peace in and for the said county by Benjamin Jinnings No. 7 Middle row Holborn in the Parish of Saint Andrew in the county of Middlesex Yeoman on the Tenth Day of this Instant Month of September at the Parish of Saint Mary Lambeth in the said county unlawfully did permit and suffer more than Six Persons that is to say nine persons to ride at the same time as outside passengers on the roof of a certain stage coach called the Kingston and Wandsworth stage coach

then and there travelling for hire and of which stage
coach you the said James Cheriston then and was proprietor and owner and then and there driven by and
under the conduct of you the said James Cheriston contrary to the statute made in the twenty eight year of the
Reign of King George the third for limiting the number
of persons to be carried on the outside of stage coaches
or other carriages which hath imposed a forfeiture of
four pounds for the said offence for every person so exceeding the number of six. These are therefore to require
you personally to appear befor me the said Justice or
such other of his Majesty's Justices as may be then and
there present on the 28 day of this instant month of
September at the hour of Eleven o'clock in the forenoon
at Union hall in the said county to answer to the said
complaint and information made by the said Benjamin
Jinnings who is likewise directed to be then and there
present to make good the same. Herein fail not. Given
under my hand and seal this 26th day of September One
thousand eight hundred and four.

John Pinkhorn

The greatest of all informers was Byas and he was active all
over the country during the 1820s, but the coming of the
railways put the informers out of business.

The carriers' Act of 1830 was 'an Act for the more effectual
protection of mail contractors stage coach proprietors, and
other Common Carriers for hire, against the loss of, or injury
to, parcels or packages delivered to them for conveyance or
custody, the value and contents which shall not be declared
to them by the owners thereof'. This important Act came
onto the statute book arising from the practice of sending
'articles of great value in small compass' by the public mails,
stage coaches, and other public conveyances by land for hire
without declaring the nature of the contents. This had led

to the common carriers becoming exposed to great and un-
avoidable risks from which some had sustained heavy losses.
This included many items such as coins, banknotes, precious
stones, paintings etc which if the value exceeded £10 for the
property contained in the parcel, the mail contractor, stage
coach proprietor, or other common carrier would not be
liable for loss or injury unless the nature of the goods had
been declared beforehand and an excess charge paid. Various
notices had to be displayed in the carrier's office and receipts
and signatures exchanged when such a package was handed
in for transit. Altogether a very important Act from the point
of view of all concerned and it is still in operation today.

By an Act of 1839 the licence duties on stage coaches (by
now termed stage carriages, a term still used to define the
bus) were related to a mileage rate dependent upon how
many passengers the coaches were licensed to convey. In 1838
mileage duty paid £166,625, mileage run 40,530,000. Still
later the mileage rate was reduced to $1\frac{1}{2}$d irrespective of
number of passengers, stage carriage licence reduced from
£5 to £3 3s and licence for coachmen or guard from £1 5s to
5s. During 1841 a mileage levy for passengers carried was
introduced together with a £3 3s licence fee for a vehicle
which exceeded 4mph.

Compared with today the number of persons who travelled
was still relatively small, particularly when one takes into
account present day travel by land, sea and air to which must
be added the enormous growth of private transport in the
last two decades. Fares on the whole were expensive but this
is understandable in relation to the number of staff who had
to be employed. In 1819 it cost a guinea inside and 10s outside
to travel from London to Ipswich whereas the coach fare
today ranges between £1 in winter and 22s in summer—it is
even cheaper if a return ticket is purchased.

CHAPTER FIVE

THE DEVELOPMENT OF THE ROADS

THROUGHOUT THE seventeenth century the state of the roads grew steadily worse, there was no system of repair, no recognised authority responsible for seeing to them, and wheeled traffic was increasing every year but in many cases could only be used on the roads in summer months. Attempts to rectify the position were sporadic. Legislation under Charles II permitted carts and waggons with four wheels and drawn by ten or more horses to carry loads of 60 or 70 cwt so we are not surprised to learn that it was a common experience to be caught fast in a quagmire. Yet for a variety of reasons, reform was resented. However, before the eighteenth century it would not have been possible, technically or economically, to construct a system of good roads throughout the country. Travellers still found it easier to go by pack horse or on the navigable rivers. Between Kensington and London as late as 1743 coaches were often bogged. Increased traffic in the middle of the eighteenth century caused further damage to the roads, which were mended by raking mud on to them and throwing faggots and boulder stones on to that base. The damage caused by the passage of vehicles resulted in protests against heavily weighted waggons rather than pressure to better the inept conditions and repair of the roads. Improvements were eventually brought about by private enterprise. Turnpike Trusts came into existence, whereby a wealthy man, or group of men, received the right of controlling a stretch of road, which was put into order and maintained in a more or less satisfactory condition. The turnpike was a gate across a road, the object being to enable tolls to be collected from users. When the bill was paid the gate was turned. When the first Turnpike Act of 1633 authorised gates on the Great North Road, so that tolls might be collected for the repair of roads in Hertfordshire, Cambridgeshire and Huntingdonshire, there arose such a public outcry that this system was crippled for the rest of the century and the battle of the Turnpike Trust had begun. Despite the many problems associated with turnpike roads they eventually resulted in road improvements and the establishment of new roads, although in many instances their construction and conditions left a great deal to be desired.

To facilitate the beginnings of the Industrial Revolution in 1760 improvement was essential, and as circumstances grew worse the government passed some two thousand road acts in connection with the Turnpike Trusts and their method of working. So from 1766 a series of Turnpike Acts began, containing clauses by which narrow wheels were penalised and broad ones relieved. A width of 16in for waggon wheels was very generally urged and adopted. Tolls were not uniform throughout the country, but although the tolls one Trust would be authorised to levy might for some special circumstance be higher than others, they ranged within narrow limits. Generally a four-wheeled waggon drawn by four horses with wheels of a less breadth than 6in would pay 1s on passing a turnpike gate: with wheels measuring 6in broad and upwards the toll would be 9d: with a breadth of 9in and upwards 6d. No one appreciated that greater haulage power would be required and consequently larger teams of horses. It was the roads which needed to be improved and as we shall note again and again in this history it was the case then as now.

The coaches were disapproved of; so were the new fangled turnpike roads. The waggoners to a man were alleged to have been opponents and a report of a conversation with the 'most solemn waggoner' on the road between London and Bath is alleged to have brought forth the comment that—

Roads were for waggon-driving; that he required but five feet width in a lane (which he resolved never to quit) and all the rest might go to devil. That the gentry ought to stay at home an be darnned and noot men gossiping up and down the country. No turnpike, no improvements of roads for him. The scripture for him was Jeremiah vi.16: Stand ye in the ways, and see, and ask for the old paths, where is the good way, and walk therein, and ye shall find rest for your souls.

Thus reports the writer 'finding Jack an ill-natured brute and a profane country way, I left him dissatisfied'.

The improvement in road construction during the eighteenth and nineteenth centuries can be attributed in the main to the work of Metcalf (1717–1810), Macadam (1756–1836) and Telford (1757–1834). Metcalf the pioneer generally worked in the North of England and his emphasis on good foundations and drainage was of particular importance. Macadam and Telford added to this with a rolled properly cambered surface of accurately graded and shaped stones. Telford, who brought sound engineering principles into road construction, paid great attention to his gradients. In particular they demonstrated that good roads could be constructed with simple materials and tools provided that the work was done with care in accordance with the specifications. Macadam, after administering roads in Scotland, moved to Bristol and the surrounding area. Both in Britain and Europe Telford had experience of building canals and commercial road building in the Highlands of Scotland. Prior to this General Wade had built a system of well-engineered military roads after the suppression of the Jacobite Rebellions in 1715 and 1745, which had brought the English as occupying force. As there were no roads for riding or marching, General Wade instructed a sapper, Captain Birt, to build roads linking the main garrison towns, having been commissioned by the government to carry out a survey of communications in Scotland. Telford's best known achievements are his bridge over the river Tay and the famous suspension bridge which carries part of the present A5 road from London to Holyhead. This road was surveyed and built in its original form under Telford's direction and when completed passed through twenty-three separate Turnpike Trusts and cost £750,000 including the cost of erecting the Menai Bridge. Telford also helped found the society which became the Institute of Civil Engineers.

As late as 1770, when the turnpike system was firmly established, Arthur Young, the agriculturalist, considered that the roads in Lancashire were fit only for horsemen.

I know not in the whole range of language, terms sufficiently expressive to describe this infernal road. Let me most seriously caution all travellers who may accidently propose to travel this terrible country to avoid it as they would the devil; for a thousand to one they break their necks or their limbs by overthrows or breakings down. They will here meet with ruts which I actually measured,

LUDLOW
SECOND TURNPIKE.

TABLE
OF TOLLS.

FOR every Coach, Chariot, Landau, Berlin, Chaise, Hearse, Calash, or other such like Carriage, drawn by Six Horses or other Beasts	}	0 2 0
And drawn by Four Horses or other Beasts - - -		0 1 6
And drawn by Two Horses or other Beasts - - -		0 0 9
And drawn by One Horse or other Beast - - -		0 0 6
FOR every Waggon, or other Four wheel Carriage, having the Fellies of the Wheels of the breadth or gage of 16 Inches, or having the Fellies of the Wheels of the breadth or gage of 9 Inches, and rolling a Surface of 16 Inches on each side thereof, drawn by Eight Horses or other Beasts	}	0 0 9
FOR every Waggon or Four-wheel Carriage, having the Fellies of the Wheels of the breadth or gage of 6 inches or upwards, and not rolling a surface of 16 Inches as aforesaid, drawn by Six Horses or other Beasts		0 1 6
FOR every Cart or other Two-wheel Carriage, having the Fellies of the Wheels of the breadth or gage of 9 Inches, drawn by any number of Horses or other Beasts, not exceeding five, or having the Fellies of the Wheels of the breadth or gage of 6 inches, and drawn by Four Horses or other Beasts - - - - - - - -		0 0 9
FOR every Waggon, or other Four-wheel Carriage, having the Fellies of the Wheels of less breadth or gage than 6 Inches, and drawn by Four Horses or other Beasts	}	0 1 6
FOR every Cart or other Two-wheel Carriage, having the Fellies of the Wheels of less breadth or gage than 6 Inches, drawn by Three Horses or other Beasts - - - - - - - -		0 1 0
And drawn by Two Horses or other Beasts - - -		0 0 9
And drawn by One Horse or other Beast - - - -		0 0 4
FOR every HORSE, MARE, GELDING, MULE, ASS, or other Beast of burthen, laden, or unladen, and not drawing - - -	}	0 0 1½

FOR every drove of Oxen, Cows, or neat Cattle, the Sum of *One Shilling & Three Pence* per Score,
And so in Proportion for any greater or less number.

And for every drove of CALVES, SWINE, SHEEP, LAMBS or GOATS, the Sum of Ten Pence per Score, and so in Proportion for any greater or less number.

Printed at the Office of H. PROCTER, Broad-street, Ludlow.

Fig 3 Table of tolls, Ludlow second turnpike

four feet deep and floating with mud only from a wet summer. What, therefore, must it be after a winter? The only mending it receives is tumbling in some loose stones which serve no other purpose than jolting the carriage in the most intolerable manner. These are not only opinions, but facts; for I actually passed three carts broken down in these eighteen miles of execrable memory.

He was equally critical of roads in South Wales:

...the turnpikes as they have the assurance to call them and the hardiness to make one pay for? From Chepstow to the halfway house between Newport and Cardiff they continue mere rocky lanes full of hugeous stones as big as one's horse, and abominable holes. The first six miles from Newport they were so detestable, and without either direction posts or milestones, that I could not well persuade myself that I was on a turnpike, but had mistook the road, and therefore asked everyone I met, who answered me, to my astonishment, 'Ya-as'.

Writing at the end of the eighteenth century, Sydney Smith records that it took him nine hours to go from Taunton to Bath and that on the journey he suffered 'between ten thousand and twelve thousand severe contusions'. But the system developed and by the nineteenth century there were some twenty thousand miles of Turnpike, some eight thousand toll gates and many of the roads had marker posts and stones (made compulsory by the Turnpike Acts of 1766 and 1773) showing the distance between the towns.

The administrative methods of the period were unable to prevent fraud and irregular practices in the operation of the turnpikes and public resentment at the extortion and dishonesty would on occasion lead to violence. The introduction of turnpiked roads towards the middle of the eighteenth cen-

Page 89 (above) Post Office, St Martins-le-Grand; *(below)* monument to mail coach men near Moffat

Page 90 Blunderbuss, pistols, mail bag and timepiece

tury was violently resisted and armed groups of men went about smashing the gates and burning down the toll houses. Pike men were attacked and even murdered. A mob from Yeadon and Otley demolished a dozen gates and at Selby the public bellman called the inhabitants to destroy the gates. But the most serious incidents occurred in June 1753, when a great number of rioters marched from Leeds to destroy the newly erected turnpike gate at Harewood Bridge. A Mr Lascelles assembled a defending force of some 300 men and at the resultant battle they beat off the rioters taking thirty prisoners, ten of whom were held in York Castle. But matters did not end here and a week later it was necessary to call on the military to defend the turnpikes in the district. Three men were arrested and imprisoned and the rioters attempted to free them. An ugly scene developed outside the Old King's Arms in Briggate, Leeds, where the magistrates and turnpike trustees sat at that time. The Riot Act was read but matters only deteriorated with the result that the troops opened fire leaving eight rioters dead and forty wounded, many of whom died. After this unfortunate sequence of events matters settled down and the roads began to be improved. It was not, however, the end of violence. This broke out from time to time, culminating in the 'Rebecca' riots in South Wales in 1842–3. They derived their name from a reference in Genesis 24:60, in which Isaac's wife is promised that her descendants will 'possess the gate of those which hate them'. With their leaders dressed in women's clothes the rioters smashed and burned turnpike gates and toll houses. Fortunately for those caught authority was aware of the injustices of the system and they received lenient treatment. From this time onward official opinion changed and in 1864 Parliament formed the House of Commons turnpike committee, which set about cutting out the number of toll bridges and roads. The coachman on the road to Buntingford had his point of view about the road makers: 'They talk of levelling the roads through the top of

F

Reed Hill, don't they coachman?' 'Oh! yes: they torkes, and that's about all they does do. Lot o' good torking does my 'orse. Vot I vants to know is. V'y does we pay the turnpikes?'

The old England of coaching days was one with never ending horizons, solid unostentatious comfort for stay at homes, but much discomfort for the traveller. This was the era when suburbs were only known around London and these were sparse. Merchants and shopkeepers still lived over their business premises. In 1787 Bloomsbury was a fashionable but rural district of London and although the City was only fifteen minutes' ride in a hackney coach cows were still driven over the cobbled streets of this elegant square. Fish Street Hill was the southerly route out of London as it connected with the old London Bridge erected in 1175, which was not replaced until 1831 when it was sited some hundreds of yards further up the Thames. This cobbled thoroughfare still exists, although as a narrow one way street. In the days of coaching it was able to handle far more traffic, private drags, herdsmen and their flocks, ladies and gentlemen on horseback and others who travelled in their own small gigs. Drays and waggons, with the carters walking beside them, were all part of a scene which was familiar to users of the City thoroughfares, which were flanked by taverns and shops identified for the imbiber and shopper by the sign swinging outside.

The rural scene was different and at the middle of the eighteenth century not nearly so comfortable as portrayed by latter-day illustrators. It was a period of violence, greed and hypocrisy and lack of communication was paradoxically a help and a hindrance to improvement, for when coaching began new liberalising ideas were able to circulate but at the same time so was avarice and vice. Pedlars travelling the countryside had been one source of news and a painting by Hogarth caricatures a pedlar selling his wares at a country inn among candidates canvassing for votes—and bribing electors—during the 1754 parliamentary campaign. Coaches arriving in villages during the summer would often have to thread their way through groups of local ale-swilling rustics, but the coachman would have to be careful where he flicked his whip to make a passage in case by chance it alighted on the local squire and gentry, who also attended these traditional summer events to lay wagers on the donkey races, which were a feature of these fairs.

By 1807 the Industrial Revolution had changed the landscape and the appearance of town and countryside. Birmingham was usually covered with a pall of smoke and the streets of brick hovels built to house the workers in the new factories were blackened with the smoke which continuously belched forth from their chimneys. Ragged children swarmed in the streets which were undermined by coal mines which, according to one coachman, 'had taken fire many years ago and still continued to burn. If you were to travel this road by night, sir,' he said, 'you would see the whole country afire, and might fancy you were going to hell!' Wolverhampton and the Potteries were reported to have been similar as indeed were other manufacturing towns. It was an England of curious and violent customs and travellers passing through London may well have seen offenders for perjury and forgery pilloried at Charing Cross where there was enough space for spectators to hurl missiles and rotten vegetables at the unfortunate victims, often with fatal results. Women with unruly tongues were fastened in a chair at the end of a long plank and plunged in and out of water until they were supposedly cured. Newcastle-under-Lyme had a variation; after a bridle and bit were placed in the mouth of the woman to curb her tongue, she would be led through the streets as an object of public ridicule.

The countryside was still pastoral but the roads were changing and new houses were being built. Coach passengers would see the milk maids driving their cows along the lanes but such had travel developed that the casual foot traveller was a person to be suspected, pitied and shunned. The roads, although dusty in summer, were lined with hedges and meadows and copses, forest and parkland were interspersed with cultivated ground. People bathed in the rivers and the long quiet twilight of an English summer evening was only disturbed by the clatter of the coaches and the guards' horns signalling the progress to the innkeepers and turnpike keepers. Road traffic beside the mail and stage coaches consisted of waggons, carts, private drags and vehicles of all descriptions; in addition to the herds of cattle, there were tinkers, gipsies, sailors travelling to join their ships, and, during the Napoleonic period, soldiers marching to defend the Dorset coast against possible invasion.

Urged by the growth of road transport, Thomas Telford surveyed a new highway, between London and Northumberland, to replace the Great North Road. He spent nearly five years on the survey between 1824 and 1829, and the work was almost completed, when news arrived of a semi-literate Northumberland mining engineer's brilliant feats with machines known as steam locomotives. It was almost another 150 years before Telford's vision of a fine new highway to the north, albeit only as far as Leeds, came into being. We call it the M1.

CHAPTER SIX

THE ROYAL MAIL

'The mail,' shouts the boy, his head out of the window. You can hear it coming up behind. The woman pulls her son towards her, so that all can see as well as hear. There it is, black and maroon, with the royal arms. No racing here. The Telegraph, your coach, gives way as a matter of precedence. And straight through the turnpike without paying. The mail rattles ahead, horn blazing. Soon your guard joins in the blare. He has as much right as the mail guard to warn the turnpike keeper.

LONG BEFORE wheeled conveyances of any kind were to be hired in this country, travellers were accustomed to ride post—post office and custom of riding post obtain their name from this common origin. The earliest date for travelling post seems to have been in the reign of Henry VIII, when the office of 'Master of the Postes' was established. 'Master of the Postes' was entrusted with arrangements for securing relays of horses for use of despatch riders, who went on affairs of state and the four post roads then organised were: London to Dover for cross channel, London to Plymouth where the king's dockyard was situated, London to Scotland and London to Chester for Ireland.

By the time of Elizabeth I messengers, as a favour, conveyed letters given into their charge for delivery on line of their journey but the post horse system was abused by travellers pretending to be on the queen's business; this kind of abuse was suppressed in 1603 after James I had come to the English throne, by a typical bureaucratic measure—a form. No person was to be supplied with horses by postmasters unless his application was supported by a document signed by one of the officers of state. Horses could, however, be hired at a rate of $2\frac{1}{2}$d per mile with a small charge for the guide. If post houses had insufficient horses for those persons on official business constables and magistrates were empowered to seize those of private owners and impress them into service.

Post masters, who were generally innkeepers on main roads, were salaried officials paid from 6d to 3s per day as a retaining fee and who, in addition, were permitted to let out horses to others riding post horse and guide about their private business. The private and unofficial travellers had to negotiate a rate between themselves and the post master, but in general, government rate was applied. Besides the hire charge, it was usual to give the guide a few pence on parting—usually a four penny piece called 'the guide's groat'. It was cheaper and safer for travellers to go together but in all cases the rider needed strength and ability to endure the fatigue. In March 1603, for example, Robert Cary (afterwards Earl of Monmouth), eager to be first to acclaim James VI of Scotland as James I of England, left London as soon as the last breath had left the body of Queen Elizabeth I; he rode the 401 miles to Edinburgh in three days.

In 1635 Thomas Witherings was appointed Master of the Posts and until he reorganised the posts there existed no

official means by which letters could be sent about the country, and to add insult to injury private persons had been
forbidden in 1603 to make the carrying of letters a business.
Like many laws this seemed made only to be broken every
day. Under Witherings's reorganisation the postmasters began
to deal with letters and in 1657 the 'Post Office of England'
was established by Act of Parliament. The office of Master
of Posts was succeeded by the newly created office of Post-
Master General whose business was defined as the exclusive
right of carrying letters and the furnishing of post horses.
These two functions, officially known for generations afterwards as the letter post and travelling post, the long line of
post-masters general continued to exercise for 123 years. In
1660 it was enacted that travellers could obtain horses from
whatever source they chose if the postmaster could not supply
within half an hour. The power of press of horses was also
repealed by the same Act. As stage coaching developed the
hiring of horses declined, for when travellers could be conveyed without exertion by coach at from 2d to 3d per mile,
they were unlikely to prefer to pay the same rate and a guide's
groat every 10 miles for the privilege of bumping in the
saddle all day. Those who mostly continued in the saddle
were the gentlemen who owned horses or those to whom the
chance company of a coach was objectionable. But it was not
until the first decade of the nineteenth century that the horse-
man disappeared from the road.

The Post Office monopoly in post horses was not worth
preserving when it was relinquished in 1780 by an Act of
Parliament. From this time on the Post Office obtained extra
revenue by the new licence duties levied upon horse keepers, postmasters and coaches. A penny a mile was fixed as the
government duty upon horses let out for hire, whether as
saddle horses or to be used in post chaises. All persons who
made this their business—generally innkeepers—were to take
out an annual 5s licence and were under obligation to pre-

sent in some conspicuous place on their houses 'Licensed to let Post Horse', in default of which the penalty was £5. As a check upon the business done, travellers hiring post horses were to be given a ticket, on which the number of horses so hired, and the distance travelled, were to be specified. These tickets were handed to the turnpike keeper at the first gate and the diligence of the officials was ensured by allowing 3d in the pound on all tickets collected. At certain periods the tickets were delivered to the stamp office and the innkeeper and postmasters themselves were visited by revenue officers who required to see the counterfoil and books from which the tickets had come.

Long before the last quarter of the eighteenth century the time was ripe for Post Office reform in the carrying of the mails. Ralph Allen, a Cornishman living in Bath, introduced a service of post boys in 1719, as usual against much opposition, riding with the mail at not less than 5mph. As the roads improved it was usual to 'post down' from London to Bath by post chaise in one day whereas it took the post boy 38 hours. The post boys went everywhere and the complex system of bye- and cross-posts established and maintained by Allen was a wonderful achievement, but Post Office revenue was suffering to the tune of £80,000 per year as a result of the unauthorised conveyance of letters in a clandestine manner by stage coach. People made up letters as parcels, preferring the comparative reliability and safety of the stage coach to the unreliability of the post boys, who were both slow and subject to all the hazards of the roads at that time, not the least of which were the highwaymen. When people grew indignant that every common traveller passed the King's Mail—there came to the fore a man to remedy the ridiculous position of government reserving to itself the monopoly of letter-carrying but not providing reasonable means for their conveyance.

This man with his revolutionary scheme of reform was John

Palmer, a native of Bath. Born in 1742 the son of a brewer and proprietor of two highly prosperous theatres in Bath and another in Bristol, he entered the theatrical business in which he was successful, making influential friends including the Hon J. J. Pratt, Lord Camden's son, MP for Bath 1790–4 and the playwright Sheridan, Secretary of the Treasury 1783. Owing to the decline of business during the American War, Palmer was financially embarrassed when, following Allen's conspicuous example, he became a 'projector'. His own frequent journeys had shown him the possibilities and his business activities had demonstrated the inadequacies of the post-boy system. Palmer proposed that a service of mail coaches should be established on every main road to be operated by contractors with the government paying them at the same rate as the post boys, exempting the coaches from tolls, and to permit passengers to be carried to provide additional revenue and profit to the contractors. The mail coaches, he proposed, should travel at 8mph, with no outside passengers but with an armed guard for the protection of the mails. The journey from London to Bath, it was thought, could be performed in sixteen hours, including stops. In the autumn of 1782 Camden introduced him to Pitt, Chancellor of the Exchequer, who encouraged the development of his plan. So did the coalition government of 1783 requiring reports from the Post Office, the staff of which were naturally opposed to a plan offending their pride and threatening their influence. Pitt then went out of office and it was not until 1784, when he was back in office again, that Palmer's plan regained favour. It is interesting that the proposal should come from outside the Post Office, whose surveyors were unanimously opposed to the scheme. One was unable to see why the mail should go by the swifter means of transport available and another thought that arming the coachman and guard would encourage the highwaymen to greater use of pistols, so that murder would be added to robbery and the scheme would end with blood. Their reports condemned it, coaches could only be used on the best roads, would be delayed by halts for passengers; would dislocate the bye- and cross-posts. Acceleration was practicable but not by this means. Their objections, though far from frivolous, received little attention from the Treasury, Sheridan observing that it was Mr Todd's (Secretary at the Post Office 1762–5, 1768–98) interest to maintain the old system. He told Palmer in August to proceed with his plan without fearing the effect of 'all the interested information from the Office and Mr Todd's representations as the plan would be adopted the following year'; the final decision being taken at a Treasury conference on 21 June. As Pitt was in favour it was carried into effect and an order published on 24 July, which stated that

His Majestys Postmaster General being inclined to make an experiment for the more expeditious conveyance of mails of letters by stage coaches, machines etc. have been pleased to order that a trial should be made upon the road between London and Bristol to commence at each place on Monday 2 August next.

On 31 July 1784 five innkeepers, one each in London, Thatchem and Marlborough and two in Bath, agreed to provide horses down the turnpike. They were to be paid 3d a mile. An advertisement to the public appeared on the same date in the *Banner and Middletons Bristol Journal* (the original style is retained but the spelling updated to modern usage):

MAIL DILIGENCE
To commence Monday, 2 August.
The proprietors of the above carriage having agreed to convey the mail to and from London and Bristol in sixteen hours, with a guard for its protection, respectfully inform the public that it is constructed so as to accom-

modate four inside passengers in the most convenient manner; that it will set off each night at eight o'clock from the Swan with Two Necks, Lad Lane, London, and arrive at the Three Tuns Inn, Bath, before ten the next morning, and at the Rummer Tavern near the Exchange, Bristol, at Twelve —— will set off from the said tavern at Bristol at four o'clock every afternoon, and arrive at London at eight o'clock the next morning. The price to and from Bristol, Bath and London 28s for each passenger —— no outside allowed.

Both the guards and coachman (who will be likewise armed) have given ample security for their conduct to the proprietors, so that those ladies and gentlemen, who may please to honour them with their encouragement, may depend on every respect and attention.

Parcels will be forwarded agreeable to the directions immediately on their arrival at London, etc etc and the price of the porterage as well as the carriage on the most reasonable terms, will be charged on the outside to prevent imposition.

Any person having reason to complain of the porter's delay, will oblige the proprietors by sending a letter of times of delivery of their parcels to any of the different inns the Diligence puts up at.

Performed by:

Wilson & Co London
Williams & Co Bath

NB The London, Bath and Bristol coaches from the above Inns as usual.

Stage-coach proprietors in general were alarmed and angered by the inauguration of a swift service of subsidised mail coaches, not only claiming to perform their journeys in a specific time, but actually doing so under contracts providing for penalties when the official timetable was not kept. They were under no such obligations and continually claimed to do things impossible to be performed, secure from penalties.

First mail coaches were ordinary light post coaches but unlike those of the other coaches whose stages ranged from 10 to 15 miles or more, the horses were changed at stages varying from 6 to 8 miles. With a speed of 8mph the Post Office was once again in the forefront and passengers flocked to the mail coaches which offered the safest and fastest means of transport. Postal charges increased but all shared the advantage of the daily service including Sundays, the reliability and the comparative immunity from attack. The residents of communities away from the mail routes were not so well served, and it was another ten years before they were connected into the network and enjoyed the same speedy service. When this was accomplished leakage of Post Office revenue automatically disappeared. Postage rates were 2d for first stage, two stages cost 3d and distances exceeding two stages and not more than 80 miles were rated at 4d.

Expansion was rapid and the next mail coach to be introduced in March 1785 was the Norwich mail followed in the May by the first cross-country mail coaches between Bristol and Portsmouth. Then in rapid succession came the Leeds, Manchester and Liverpool on 25 July; the London, Gloucester and Swansea; the Hereford, Carmarthen and Milford Haven; the Worcester and Ludlow; the Birmingham and Shrewsbury; the Chester and Holyhead (a road having been opened to the port in 1783); the Exeter; the Portsmouth; and—on 16 October 1786—the York and Edinburgh Mail. To honour Palmer the Bristol coach took precedence over its fellows when the cavalcade left London every night.

The first mail coach in Cornwall commenced on 9 July 1799 between Falmouth via Launceston to Exeter, where mail for London was transferred to the Exeter–London coach. So important did Falmouth become as a packet station that the north road via Launceston and the south road via Torpoint quickly developed as being amongst the most important in the country. Several branch mails operated to connect up with the main routes and for many years mail coaches without horses were ferried across the Tamar on the Torpoint ferry, but when in 1834 a new steamer ferry was introduced it was considered sufficiently reliable for the coaches to cross without changing horses. In fact the 'floating bridge' arrangement of the ferry provided for sufficient space to convey four coaches with four horses each at the same time. The charge was 5s for a coach and four and double on Sundays. With this improved facility the Quicksilver Mail which ran between London and Devonport was extended via the Torpoint Ferry to Falmouth.

Success had not come easily and in the early days a dispute over the rival merits of carts and coaches developed into a bitter administrative struggle between the Secretary supported by the Post Office and the projector supported by the Treasury. In the autumn of 1785 the Post Office made a great effort to ruin the plan by obstruction and the use of carts. Concentrating on the Portsmouth road, Todd caused confusion by interfering with the schedules and running carts in competition. In February 1786 the new schedules were condemned by a meeting of London merchants obliged to post mail by evening instead of midnight. On 1 March the Board of the Post Office sent its final report to the Treasury condemning coaches and commending carts. Palmer sent a final appeal to Pitt on 26 April 1786 blaming Todd personally for all his difficulties.

On 5 August 1786 Pitt by Treasury warrant ordered the Board to give Palmer the promised place, salary and poundage and on 11 October the Board appointed Palmer Controller General, though without the poundage because of doubts concerning its legality. Palmer, embarrassed by debts, took office on Pitt's promise that it would be settled later. So at last Palmer had achieved his objective and settled the inland posts. Palmer's appointment was followed by a long pitiful story of hatreds and jealousies and he quickly came into conflict with the postmasters general. The outcome was a violent quarrel with Palmer charging the postmasters general with deliberately and capriciously thwarting his best arrangements. The matter was referred to the prime minister and despite Pitt's great regard for Palmer he could not ignore letters written in confidence and treacherously disclosed. Palmer was dismissed but he did not go without acknowledgement and his salary and commission which had reached £3,000 a year was continued to him as a pension from 1792, the date of his dismissal. The matter did not end there and for the full story the reader is recommended to consult K. Ellis, *The Post Office in the Eighteenth Century* (see Bibliography). Consequently, although his coaches continued to run till the railway age, his downfall in June 1792 was complete. He never did receive the poundage, finally agreeing to accept £50,000. Long after his death in 1818, ministers remembered the settlement of his claim as a warning against the encouragement of projecters.

Thomas Hasker, formerly superintendent of mail coaches, was upgraded on Palmer's departure to a newly created post of surveyor and superintendent of mail coaches. He now had complete control of the mail coach organisation which he administered with great ability, watching over the activities of the contractors, guards and coachmen. One of his first directives to the mail coach guards sums up the working of the scheme at the end of the eighteenth century:

TO THE MAIL GUARDS

When the coach is so broke down that it cannot proceed as it is on its way to London and if you have not above two passengers, and you can procure a post chaise without loss of time, get them and the mail forward in that way, with the horses that used to draw the mail coach, that they may be in their place till you come where a coach is stationed; and if you have lost any time you must endeavour to fetch it up, which may be easily done, as the chaise is lighter than the coach.

If you cannot get a post chaise, take off one of the coach horses, and ride with your bags to the next stage, there take another horse, and so on, till you come to the end of your ground, when you must deliver the bags to the next guard, who must proceed in the same manner.

The contractors will be paid for their horses by the office, the same as they pay for expresses, 3d per mile.

If your mail is so large (as the York, Manchester, and two or three are at some part of the road) that one horse cannot carry it, you may take two, tie the mail on one horse and ride the other.

The person who horses the mail, must order his horse keeper at every stage to furnish you with horses in case of accidents.

Change your bags regularly at every post town, and do all your office duty the same as if the coach travelled.

If in travelling from London, an accident happens, use all possible expedition in repairing the coach to proceed; and if it cannot be repaired in an hour or two, take the mail forward by horse or chaise, and if the latter the passengers will go with it.

By command of the postmaster general,

THOMAS HASKER,
Superintendent of mails.

The earliest mail coaches were not up to the fast running and although the coaches were supplied by the contractors the Post Office was very closely interested in their efficiency. In 1787, Palmer complained to the contractors not only of the quality of the horses on the Bristol mail, but also of the harness and the accoutrements in use. He arranged for new sets of harness to be supplied for which the contractors had to pay, and at this time a set of harness cost fourteen guineas. The next step was the coach itself and the Post Office's approved type was a 'patent coach' weighing 16cwt designed

Page 107 (above) Swan with Two Necks, Lad Lane; (below) the Lioness attacking the Quicksilver at the Pheasant Inn, Winterdow (engraved by R. Harvell)

Page 108 The Cambridge Telegraph coach loaded with undergraduates outside the White Horse Tavern, Fetter Lane (*engraved by G. Hunt*)

by Besant, the use of which was made a condition of contract.

Besant's patent mail coach came on the road in 1787. At first from want of system these coaches were often sent out without being greased and generally even without being washed or cleaned. Besant died in 1791 and in 1792 **Palmer** entered into an arrangement with Vidler, a coach builder who established a coach building establishment at Millbank, Westminster, from which mail coaches were supplied for the next forty years to the mail contractors. At this time there were 120 coaches for which Vidler charged $2\frac{1}{2}$d per double mile inclusive of maintenance and repair. Vidler's men took over the mail coaches upon arrival at the General Post Office and drove them to Millbank for cleaning and greasing. The coaches spent two days at Millbank for this service for which Vidler charged 1s. This raised objections from the coach masters who were required to pay the 1s and in the end the Post Office agreed to meet the charge.

The Besant 'patent coach' was regarded as a most uncomfortable vehicle to ride in and in 1798 Matthew Boulton, speaking of a mail coach journey to Exeter, stated that:

The landlady in the London Inn at Exeter [a modern public house—the London Inn—now stands on the site] assured me that the passengers who arrived every night were in general so ill they were obliged to go supperless to bed; and unless they go back to old fashioned coaches, long and a little lower, the mail coaches will lose all their custom.

In answer to a question Palmer said, 'They are all driven with four horses, sometimes in snow and bad weather with six; never less than four whether they have passengers or not.'

Seldom a day went by without a wheel catching fire or collapsing and 21 September 1796 Hasker wrote to Vidler:

The sudden wet weather has an effect on wheels no

G

doubt. The near fore wheel of the Newmarket coach and
both fore wheels of the Ipswich broke this morning. I
must beg you will order your people to pay particular
attention to the wheels and send [them] out very perfect
this night.

Eventually an easily changeable wheel hub with three
taper bolts was developed for the mail coaches and spare
wheels were kept at strategic points. Vidler retained the contract for the supply of mail coaches until 1836, when the Post
Office decided to put it out to tender dividing the country
into three districts. Vidler's tender to

furnish efficient carriages for the conveyance of His
Majesty's mail for the southern, midland and northern
divisions, to be employed not less than 90 single miles
daily, including every expense of drawing them to and
from their respective Inns for oiling and greasing them
for a period of seven years at $2\frac{1}{2}$d per double mile

was not accepted. Instead the postal authorities chose Wright,
Home & Williams for the southern and midland districts at
$2\frac{1}{2}$d the double mile, and Croall & Wallace for the northern
districts at 2d per double mile. The contractors experienced
difficulty with the Croall coaches alleging they were heavy,
clumsy and defective, which was in general confirmed in a
report of the Post Office inspectors dated 19 June 1839. Croall
was required to refurbish the coaches not up to standard and
to reduce all those coaches whose weight was in excess of 8cwt.

The contractors who horsed the coaches were chosen by the
Post Office after an investigation of the background of the
applicants. Contracts specified routes, minimum speed, and
number of passengers who could be conveyed. Innkeepers
were generally proprietors of coaches and in a circular letter
written to the contractors in 1798 the Post Office advised them
that

should you retire from the public line, you must not
expect to continue in the Mail coach concern; for so
many innkeepers are quitting their inns and retaining
possession of their coaches, that will be the cause of
bringing forward very formidable oppositions by those
persons who have taken such inns.

In 1812 the cost to an inside passenger for fare exclusive
of tips to coachmen and guards on the London–Glasgow mail
coach but excluding expenditure for food and drink was £10.
Very few passengers made through journeys at one go on the
long runs, ie London to Glasgow 404 miles, three nights, two
days, so in addition there was accommodation and meals to
be paid for.

Mails generally averaged about 7mph until the beginning
of the nineteenth century, during which running times were
accelerated resulting from improved roads. Mail coaches paid
no tolls and as the number of mail coaches increased this
became a real grievance to the Turnpike Trusts due to the
wear and tear, especially as the Post Office surveyors had
power under Act of Parliament of indicting roads in bad
condition. In certain cases the Post Office refused to commence services until new roads and short cuts had been provided to meet their requirements. So for many roads today
we owe the Post Office a debt. Again there was a disparity
between heavy and little used roads in relation to toll receipts
from other forms of traffic and, in some cases, stage coaches
using those roads had been run off by competition from the
mails.

In 1810 Turnpike Trusts approached Parliament for re-
dress of this grievance but with no success and in many
instances the adverse reports of the Post Office surveyors
resulted in heavy fines being inflicted on those trusts which
were hardest hit by mail exemptions. In the end many roads
were dispiked before the Trusts had paid off their loans and

General Post-Office.

The Earl of CHESTERFIELD, ⎱ Postmaster-
AND
The Earl of LEICESTER, ⎰ General.

London to Exeter Time-Bill.

	Miles	Time allowed H. M.	
			Dispatched from the General Post-Office, the of 179
			at
			Coach Nº sent out { With a Time-Piece safe Nº to
			Arrived at the Gloucester Coffee-house, Piccadilly, at
Wilson —	3·½	3 55	Arrived at Bagshot at *11 . 55*
Demezy —	20	2 30	Arrived at Basingstoke at *2 . 25*
W. Wilson —	8½	1 10	Arrived at Overton at *3 . 35*
Weeks —	28½	3 40	Arrived at Salisbury at *7 . 15* Delivered the Time-Piece safe to
			Coach Nº gone forward
		.30	*To be at Salisbury by a Quarter past Seven, where Thirty Minutes are allowed for Breakfast*
Shergold —	10	1 20	Arrived at Woodyeats at *9 .. 5*
Wood ·	12½	1 40	Arrived at Blandford at *10 45*
Bryer —	16	2 10	Arrived at Dorchester at *12 . 55*
		30	*Thirty Minutes allowed for Dinner, &c.*
Warre —	27½	4 0	Arrived at Axminster at *5 . 25*
Pine —	9½	1 15	Arrived at Honiton at *6 . 40*
Land —	16	2 10	Arrived at the Post-Office, Exeter, the of 179 at *8 . 50*
	179	24 50	*The Mail to be delivered at the Post-Office, Exeter, Fifty Minutes past Eight in the Evening*
			Coach Nº arrived { Delivered the Time-Piece safe Nº to

The Time of working each Stage is to be reckoned from the Coach's Arrival. Five Minutes for changing four Horses, is as much as is necessary, and as the Time whether more or less, is to be fetched up in the Course of the Stage, it is the Coachman's Duty to be as expeditious as possible, and to report the Horse-keepers if they are not always ready when the Coach arrives, and active in getting it off.

By Command of the Postmaster-General,

T. HASKER.

Fig 5 Timebill for the London–Exeter mail coach, 1797

what had been a secure and favourable form of investment now became worthless in many cases and the investors were ruined. Mail coaches continued to go free to the end in England and Wales although toll was paid from 1798 in Ireland. In Scotland an Act was passed in 1813 repealing the exemption but the Post Office added a $\frac{1}{2}$d surcharge to Scottish mail. The Turnpike Trusts responded by raising the tolls so the Post Office cut off a number of the mails and in the end won the day. An estimate prepared for Parliament in 1812 for mail exemptions in Scotland amounted to £11,229, for England £33,536, for Wales £5,224.

The mail coaches in their prime were splendid vehicles. The lower part of the body and underframe was painted scarlet; and the front and rear boots, upper panels and roof black. The whole being lined out in gold with the Royal cypher on

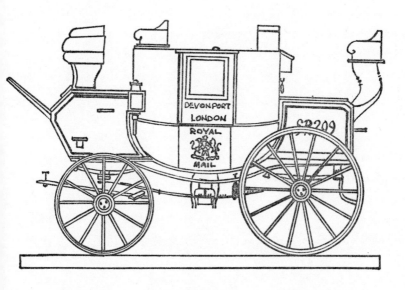

Fig 6 General arrangement sketch-drawing of mail coach

the front boot, the vehicle number on the rear boot was in gold. On the upper panels were the Cross of St George, the Scots thistle, the Shamrock and the Royal crowns. Royal arms were displayed on the door with the name of the particular mail in gold letters. Whilst there was some variation the crack mails carried five lamps (which used whale oil), four on the upper parts of the body, and another under the footboard, casting a light upon the horses' backs and harness.

From 1825 when the era of the fast day coaches began mails gradually lost their pre-eminence. They suffered the disability of night travel and the necessity to transact Post Office business on route which increased their overall journey time, despite the fact that they kept high average speeds between stages; whilst the image is of corpulent gentlemen full of good cheer, apparently enjoying the rigours of night travel, this is far from the truth. The passengers preferred to travel by day.

have developed in the way it did. Here was a ready-made institution catering for travellers on which to base the coaches, stable the horses, make changeovers of horses and coachmen, and provide rest and refreshment for passengers. New inns were specially built to accommodate the travellers and inn-keepers did a roaring trade. A whole industry grew up around coaching; each inn required its squad of barmaids, chamber-maids, cooks and waiters to attend to the traveller while ost-lers, grooms, stable lads and smiths were there to look after the horses. Furthermore there were coach builders, upholster-ers, wheelwrights, painters and body builders employed to build and maintain the coaches. Coaching inns usually had large stable yards for the coaches and high arched doorways, sometimes double for entrances and exits. In many instances the posting house was at the local inn or inns which flourished and expanded to meet the demands of the ever increasing road traffic until the railways came and swept the coaches away; then the inn reverted to being the centre of a small community, catering for the occasional traveller until the return of traffic to the roads in the form of mechanical vehicles awakened it from its slumbers. In 1799 the Post Office, in an attempt to obtain more revenue, made efforts to induce coffee-house proprietors to act as agents for the Post Office but with conspicuous lack of success, although some had a mail bag hanging up for collection of letters. If they had been suc-cessful it is interesting to speculate as to whether or not the inns would have remained the coaching centre. 'Commercial inns' began in the middle ages and by the fifteenth century the inn had become a sophisticated development of the ale house or tavern which sold only ale, bread and meat. The sophisticated inn had a sign board and varied fare.

Post boys were originally the King's Messengers who wore a bright red uniform and carried the King's mail—the Royal Mail. Later they carried mail for other persons as well and became known as post boys. Riding on horseback they were required to carry a post horn which had to be blown every 3 miles. Post houses were denoted by the post horn over the door of the inn. Letters were not delivered and had to be taken to or collected from the posting house.

With the introduction of mail coaches many of the post boys were rendered redundant and so their second function was developed, that of hire of the post chaises and post boys on a mileage basis. The post boy then became a postilion who rode one of a pair of horses attached to a post chaise. The post chaise, painted yellow and often known as the 'yellow bounder', was usually a small closed chariot capable of carrying two passengers and a limited amount of luggage. Rates for hire varied between 9d and 1s per mile on top of which it was necessary to tip. The post boys (who were usually much older than their name implies) received their keep from the innkeeper who hired them out and in the summer they could earn as much as £5 per week. Persons who travelled in this manner were said to be 'travelling post' or 'posting'. Each post boy had four horses in his charge, each pair taking regular turns, the first and second pairs being at readiness so that even if no outrider had gone ahead there was little delay in the change. A ticket was issued from the posting house which the post boy gave up at the turnpike gate making the actual payment on his return with the loose horses or the empty chaise. As most towns had more than one posting house it was the custom of the inns at which they terminated their journeys to entertain them on a scale which varied according to the amount of competition from rival inns. The average post boy was usually small in stature and required to provide his own uniform, of breeches, short top boots, a large beaver hat and in the South of England a bright yellow jacket, whereas in the North this was red. The waistcoats were striped according to the inn from which he worked. A cravat folded from two yards of white linen and a buff-coloured great coat completed his uniform. Whilst black hats were considered correct, different colours were sometimes worn to distinguish the lads where opposition posting houses were established. At Ferrybridge those from the Greyhound wore white hats whilst those from the Angel wore black. This particular inn at the height of its fame was kept by George Alderson, a doctor of medicine, coach proprietor, and innkeeper. He horsed the Highflyer and the Leeds Union from the Angel to Doncaster and two mail coaches to and from Robin Hood's Well.

Posting was not without its dangers and its fun; we learn of racing between lads from opposition houses; and danger to the post boy from passengers, one of whom threatened to shoot the post boy if he did not go faster and at journey's end refused to pay; instead he brought the lad drinks with the threat

Have another glass, you villain, or I'll shoot you. And said the lad I had all sorts o' glasses. He gev me half a soverayn at the finish. I nivver wor so filled up i' all my life afore. I fell off seven times between Doncaster an' York Bar, [about half a mile], an' then I fell asleep in t' hedge bottom, an' lost one o' t' horses. Eh, he wor a terrible customer wor that thear, bud I stuck to him an' got my brass after all.

Runaway weddings were a frequent affair on the Great North Road and it was not unknown for the same post house to supply horses for pursued and pursuer, who sometimes arrived at the stage first with the result that the elopers were caught and the girl taken home by a determined father.

There were, of course, innkeepers and innkeepers ranging from the business of William Chaplin who operated coaches from various London inns through to the small innkeeper whose prime source of income was his inn but who had a share in a coach agreeing to provide for his ground for a share of the profits. Booking offices were also installed at the inns and it is clear that the stage coach business was run from the inns. The mail-coach system depended on their existence but was controlled from the General Post Office in St Martins-le-Grand where Sherman had his Bull and Mouth inn.

The business of coach proprietor was one in which few became rich; they lived hard, worked hard, and swore hard; there never was a more speculative or competitive business. Most outstanding proprietor was William James Chaplin, son of an expanding coachman and small time coach pro-prietor. He became a practised coachman experienced in all aspects of the business including buying of horses. Centre of operations from 1825 was the Swan with Two Necks in Lad Lane (the Swan with Two Necks was originally the Swan with Two Nicks, ie a swan belonging to the Vintner's Com-pany with two nicks in its beak), where he constructed under-ground stables which housed 200 horses. In 1838 Chaplin owned or part owned 68 coaches and 1,800 horses, most of which were purchased at Horncastle Fair. He gave employ-ment to 2,000 people, and of the 27 mails out of London he horsed 14 on the first and last stages into town. Several of these were the fastest mails, amongst them the Devonport (Quicksilver), and New Holyhead and Bristol. The business's annual return was £250,000. Coach proprietors realised that they could not keep a full check on their coachmen or guards and 'shouldering' of fares and 'swallowing' of passengers was well known to them but so long as their takings reached a certain average sum they did not worry; it was only when they fell below that figure or when a fare was 'shouldered' or a passenger 'swallowed' before their eyes that trouble began. Or, as Chaplin put it, 'success to shouldering but do it well'; in other words do not get found out. His coaches were the Manchester Defiance, Birmingham Greyhound, Cambridge Magnet, Liverpool Red Rover, Bristol Emerald, Cheltenham Magnet and many others besides those in which he had half-shares including the Birmingham Tantivy. He also owned several other inns which were used as coach terminals including the Spread Eagle and Cross Keys, Gracechurch Street, together with a coach office in Regent's Circus. Chaplin's coaches went in all directions and he owned large stables at Purley, Hounslow and Whetstone. At the height of the coaching era Hounslow was the greatest coaching centre in the country where about 2,500 horses were stabled and customarily the place where west country coaches changed horses for the last time before London.

He foresightedly saw that the railways would replace coaches and, after going into association with Benjamin Worthing Horne, assisted the London & Birmingham Railway in its early days by withdrawing competition and providing feeder coaches. He obtained a share with Pickford & Co in the goods and parcel agency for the line. He then sold most of his coaches and turned these assets into cash, a large portion of which he invested in the London & Birmingham Railway, soon becoming a director and then deputy chairman in 1839; he became chairman in 1843 and with one interval was chairman until 1858 of what became the London & South Western Railway, when he was forced by ill-health to resign. He was a director of several European railways; Sheriff of London 1845–6, Member of Parliament for Salisbury 1847–57. He died in 1859 in his seventy-second year.

The other partner in the firm of Chaplin & Horne (carriers and coach operators on routes not yet affected by rail) was Benjamin Worthy Horne, whose chief centre of business was the Golden Cross, Charing Cross. He succeeded his father who died aged forty-five in 1828 having developed a very successful business which had 700 horses at coach at this time. Aged twenty-four when he took over Benjamin had fifty-six coaches departing daily. His stables were at Barnet and Finchley. Besides the Independent Tally Ho! and other coaches, he started in 1834 in alliance with two other partners the Nimrod between London and Shrewsbury, competing with one of the original long distance day coaches, Sherman's Wonder, which had commenced on this road in 1825, and the bitterness stirred up by this move was incredible; Sherman replied by introducing the Stag on the same road running slightly in front of the Nimrod with the Wonder behind. So the rival was 'nursed' with racing and fare cutting. There was a fatal accident when the coachman of the Nimrod on the Wolverhampton and Shrewsbury stage was thrown off. Sherman and his allies lost £1,500 in twelve months but the Nimrod was withdrawn. Horne was a dangerous competitor who would endeavour to run any competitor off the road if he was not prepared to co-operate with him; obviously many small proprietors found the latter course preferable but some refused and Horne, although ready to work with any proprietor, was in bitter opposition on many roads. Horne was a mail contractor and at one time had the old Chester and Holyhead; the Cambridge Auxiliary, the Gloucester and Cheltenham; the Dover foreign mail, the Norwich via Newmarket; the Milford Haven; and the Winchester and Oxford. The Bedford Times, started in 1836 by Whitbread the brewers as a hobby, was horsed out of London by Horne. It was an exclusive coach, built on the lines of a private drag and ran to the Swan Hotel at Bedford. It was one of the last surviving coaches and ran until 1848. Being an astute businessman and correctly appraising the future he obtained the parcel agency of the London & Birmingham Railway in association with William Chaplin.

Sherman ranked next to Chaplin as the largest coach proprietor in London. A broker, he established himself at the Bull and Mouth, St Martins-le-Grand, in 1823, in succession to Willian, who, it is suggested, employed 'a dissatisfied grumbling set of fellows, and their turn outs of horses and harness beggarly'. Sherman changed all that and to the discomfort of the established proprietors pioneered the fast long-

distance day coaches including the Shrewsbury Wonder referred to above, which ran 158 miles in a day at an average
speed of 11½mph. All his coaches were painted in a standard
livery of light yellow and black. His supreme achievement
was the Manchester Telegraph started in 1833 and running
186 miles in eighteen hours departing at 5am and reaching
Manchester at 11pm. This fast timing was subsequently reduced by one hour. The Telegraph day coach was specially
built by Warde, and was a long-hung vehicle with flat springs
and a low centre of gravity. The coach competed with Chaplin's Manchester Defiance which was speeded up to compete
with the Telegraph. A further coach was the Peveril of the
Peak (a night coach) which was rivalled by Robert Nelson's
Manchester Red Rover in competition on the Manchester
road. This coach had guards in red coats and the horses wore
red harness and collars on the stage into and out of London.
Sherman obtained the Red Rover and Nelson introduced a
further new coach on this road, the Beehive. The advertisement for the introduction makes interesting and significant
reading as it sums up the state of competition at this time:

NEW COACH FROM THE BEEHIVE COACH OFFICE

Merchants, buyers and the public in general visiting
London and Manchester are respectfully informed that
a new coach, called the Beehive, built, expressly, and
fitted up with supreme accommodation for comfort and
safety to any coach in Europe, will leave La Belle Sauvage, Ludgate Hill, London, at eight every morning and
arrive in Manchester the following morning, in time for
the coaches leaving for Carlisle, Edinburgh and Glasgow.
Passengers travelling to the north will reach Carlisle the
following morning, being only one night on the road.
The above coach will leave the Beehive Coach office,
Market Street, near the Exchange Manchester, every
evening at seven and arrive in London the following
afternoon at three. All small parcels sent by this convey-

ance will be delivered to the furthest part of London within two hours after the arrival of the coach. In order to insure safety and punctuality, with respectability, no large packages will be taken, or fish of any description carried by this conveyance. The inside of the coach is fitted up with spring cushions and a reading-lamp, lighted with wax, for the accommodation of those who wish to amuse themselves on the road. The inside backs and seats are also fitted up with hair cushions, rendering them more comfortable to passengers than anything hitherto brought out in the annals of coaching, and, to prevent frequent disputes respecting seats, every seat is numbered. Persons booking themselves at either of the above places will receive a card, with a number upon it, thereby doing away with the disagreeables that occur daily in the old style. The route is through Stockport, Macclesfield, Congleton, Newcastle, Wolverhampton, Birmingham, Coventry, Dunchurch, Towcester, Stony Stratford, Buckhill, Dunstable, and St Albans, being the most level line of country, avoiding the danger of the steep hills through Derbyshire.

Performed by the public's obedient servants.

ROBERT NELSON, London.

F. CLARE, Stony Stratford.

ROBERT HADLEY & CO, Manchester.

Robert Nelson was one of the sons of Mrs Ann Nelson of the Bull Inn, Whitechapel, of Exeter Telegraph fame. By the end of the coaching era Mrs Nelson had acquired the Spread Eagle in Gracechurch Street, and the Swan with Two Necks in Lad Lane. As an inn the Bull was known to the very last and as it was the starting-point for the coaches to the eastern counties she did a highly lucrative trade in hotel business. Everything at the Bull was solid and substantial and a feature was the rooms reserved exclusively for their coachmen and guards. Here the staff wined and dined as well as any travellers, on occasion entertaining distinguished guests like Sir Henry Payton, one of the well-known amateurs, and once Charles Dickens. Etiquette of the room required that the oldest coachman presided (never a guard, for they ranked as juniors) and they were always addressed in terms of the road they worked—Manchester, Devonport, Oxford etc. When Mrs Nelson retired, her son John took over and in the face of railway competition started a successful bus undertaking called the Wellington.

Thomas Fagg, a coach maker of Hartley Row near Basingstoke, was a small proprietor but he had twenty-six stage coaches going daily from his premises at the Bell and Crown, Holborn.

Another energetic lady was Mrs Maintain of the Saracen's Head, Snow Hill. She had a coach factory, building coaches for herself and others to whom she hired them at 3½d per mile. After the death of her husband she carried on the business with her only son. Thirty coaches left her inn daily including, from 1823, the first of Birmingham's Tally Ho! fast day coaches.

Robert Gray of the Bolt-in-Tun, Fleet Street, saw twenty-five coaches depart from his inn down the southern and western roads, including the Portsmouth and Hastings mails, whereas the Brighton mail operated from the Blossoms Inn, Laurence Lane, Cheapside, from where William Gilbert sent out the Birmingham Tantivy. Seventeen other coaches left his yard. Principal operator of the slow coaches, of which he had twenty-two, was Joseph Hearn, proprietor of the King's Arms, Snow Hill, amongst which was the Bicester Regular, the Boston Perseverance, and the Leicester & Market Harborough Convenience running at average speeds of 6mph. In the provinces where competition was no less bitter the famous names were Birchester, Liverpool; Wetherald, Manchester; Teacher, Carlisle; and Waddell, Birmingham.

Competition was usually extended from racing on the roads

Page 125 (above) Iain Macauley and the 'breaking-in cart' at Charlecote Carriages, Charlecote, Warwicks; (below) Crown Hotel and Posting House, Bawtry, Yorkshire

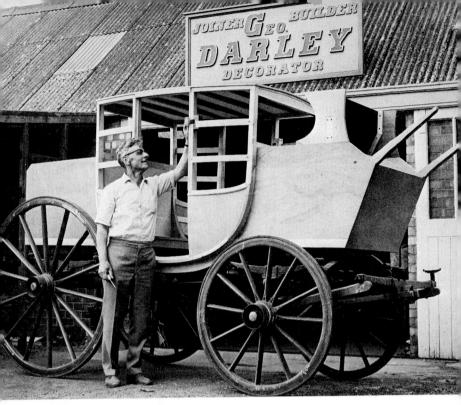

Page 126 (above) George Darley with the 'Hero' stage-coach for which he built a new body; (below) 'Hero' stage-coach on its first run with Captain Walker, the owner, driving; George Darley in bowler hat is seated behind him

to price cutting and competitive advertising. During May 1801 a price war developed on the road between London and Leeds which brought forth the following announcement from the proprietors of the True Briton:

The proprietors of the True Briton coach, impressed with a lively sense of the liberal support of a discerning public, feel themselves called upon, by an advertisement from the Bull and Mouth, to address the public at large: the reasons there held up, for offering to accommodate the public at such inadequate terms, are too gross to deceive the most ignorant in the knowledge of horse-keeping, and are intended only to injure the fair trades-man. The proprietors of the True Briton coach, there-fore, flatter themselves with a continuance of support from the public at the moderate price of £3 3s from London to Leeds and other distances in a similar propor-tion; and hereby pledge themselves to continue their conveyance in a style of expedition and care, equal to the best connection of the kind in the kingdom. Those who travel in the True Briton may depend on being treated with the best attention and genteel coaches, without being subject to the inconvenience of a carriage, made for the purpose of carrying twelve insides, which is a scheme to make up by numbers for low prices, and an imposition on the unwary, by those opponents who have not courage to contest the business at a price that will satisfy both traveller and coachmaster.
Performed by J. Robinson, London
        J. Hicks, Leeds   Old King's Arms,
                    Leeds 29 May 1801

Another similar battle developed in 1834 between two rival coaching groups, Bird, Sherman & Co and Haxwell, Hogarth, Nelson, Chaplin & Co, when the latter concern reduced their fares between London and the east coast, whereupon Bird,

H

Sherman & Co made the following announcement in the local Press:

> Stimulated by exertion by a determined opposition, the proprietors of the Magnet coach are prepared to meet the crisis with the weight of superior forces, and the support of a more extensive connection. They are grateful for past favours, and will continue to deserve them by one firm undeviating line of conduct. Passengers will receive the most marked attention and accommodation. Parcels will be delivered with the most determined promptitude, and the coach timed with the utmost punctuality.

Some of the innkeepers had an interest in all facets of the trade as is exemplified by George Clarke of the Blue Bell, Barnby Moor, in Nottinghamshire. He horsed the mails from this inn and other coaches from the White Horse inn in the same village. He had extensive stabling at the rear of the premises with numerous paddocks crowded with young stock. There was an extensive farm which supplied the stables with hay and corn and Mr Clarke was equally famous as farmer and a breeder of blood stock. He bred racehorses and those not fast enough for the turf were relegated to the road and such was his reputation that a coach proprietor remarked, 'Ah! Mr Clarke's cattle were of an exceptional character; he kept the right sort for doing the distance.' Another acquaintance of this remarkable man commented that he was 'a true sportsman, gentleman, and roadside landlord of his own school; for without disparagement...I have seldom if ever met a man in the same walk of life activated by views so enlarged or possessed of manners so perfectly unobjectionable as the gentleman landlord at whose house we remained half a day and night.'

Businesses, horses and coaches were sold in much the same way as the present motor trade and typical press advertisements in *The Times* in 1835 were:

TO COACHMEN and others — To be SOLD the very superior old-established BRIGHTON COACH. Any young man capable of driving will find it a pleasant and advantageous business. Illness of one of the partners is the cause of its being parted with. For particulars inquire of Mr Rickman, Globe tavern, Baker Street; or Mr A. Pickett, Golden Cross, Princes street, Brighton.

CARRIAGES A very superior assortment of NEW and SECOND HAND CHARIOTS fitted up either for town use or posting, may be seen at S. MARK'S and SON'S, Langham place, Cavendish square, where there is an extensive variety of carriages to be let for any period. Gentlemen having carriages to dispose of will find an advantage in sending them to this establishment for sale on commission. Invalid carriages for any journey.

TILBURY and HARNESS, price 35 guineas, painted and lined green, nearly equal to new, with patent axle tree. To be seen at Seymour's yard, Tichborne Street, Haymarket. Enquire for the ostler.

VERY CHEAP TRAVELLING TO YORK. Hull, Lincoln and Stamford, from the Belle Sauvage, Ludgate hill; 30s inside, 15s outside, every evening at half past five. JEREMIAH BRYANT, Proprietor. Also to Liverpool, Manchester, Birmingham, Wolverhampton, and Coventry; Portsmouth, Southampton, Bath, Bristol, Cheltenham, Oxford, Leamington, Leeds, Nottingham, Sheffield, Norwich, Lynn, Cambridge, Yarmouth, Ipswich, and Colchester; morning and evening. The carriage of parcels from this office is upon the most economical calculation.

Advance booking was the general rule, although last minute passengers were catered for if room. When the ticket was issued the passenger's name and details of journey were entered in the ledger and it was usual to pay half fare on booking, the remainder on taking up one's seat. The booking clerk was responsible for any errors; if it was overbooked the proprietors were bound in law to convey the excess passengers by post chaise at from 9d to 1s per mile as opposed to coach fare of 2d to 5d per mile. The clerk had to make up the difference out of his wages.

Departures on long-distance coaches travelling 100 miles or more were very early in the morning or late afternoon, starting at 5am and at varying departure times until 9pm. In 1824 the three early coaches for Bath, for instance, departed London at 5am, 5.45am and 6.15am; the first night coaches left at 3pm and thence at intervals to 9pm. Early rising was necessary to get to Sherman's Bull and Mouth, Chaplin's Swan with Two Necks, the Belle Sauvage, the Cross Keys or any inn of departure and the wise obtained rooms at the inn from which the coach commenced.

> First of all, you had in winter, to be called before day light; then you had to proceed in a rattling hackney coach (your teeth rattling to match with the cold) to the office from which the Wonder, Telegraph, Regulator, High Flyer or Independent started. Trudging to the booking office with its gas-lights and blazing fire the clerk advises you 'that the coach is up the yard'. As there is a quarter of an hour to wait a visit to 'the Tap' for a hot brandy-and-water is indicated. Somehow the kettle boils two and a half minutes before the starting time of the coach and the tap waiter enjoys your hot brandy-and-water.

Charles Dickens had no great opinion of travellers' waiting rooms:

> The travellers' room at the White Horse Cellar is of course uncomfortable; it would be no travellers' room if it were not. It is the right hand parlour, into which an aspiring kitchen fire-place appears to have walked, accom-

panied by a rebellious poker, tongs, and shovel. It is divided into boxes, for the solitary confinement of travellers, and is furnished with a clock, a looking glass, and a live waiter; which latter article is kept in a small kennel for washing glasses, in a corner of the compartment.

After the first stroke of six peals from St Martin's Church steeple, the coach is out, the luggage loaded, and the inside passengers seated and the outsides looking cold and miserable. 'Take off the cloths Bob', says the coachman who now appears for the first time, in a royal blue great coat, of which the buttons behind are so far apart that you can't see them both at the same time. 'Now gen'l'm'n!' says the guard, with the waybill in his hand. 'Five minutes behind time already.' 'All right!' sings out the guard at last jumping up, the coach starts, and blowing his horn directly afterwards, 'Let 'em go Harry; give 'em them heads' cries the coachman—and off we go.

But at all the inns the time for departure would arrive and again Charles Dickens brings the scene to life:

The Commodore was on the point of starting. 'Commodore', said the stranger, starting up, 'my coach,—place booked,—one outside—leave you to pay for the brandy and water,—want change for a five,—bad silver—Brummagem buttons—wont do—nogo—eh?' and he shook his head knowingly.

Now it so happened that Mr Pickwick and his three companions had resolved to make Rochester their first halting-place too; and having intimated to their new acquaintance that they were journeying to the same city, they agreed to occupy the seat at the back of the coach, where they could all sit together. 'Up with you,' said the stranger, assisting Mr Pickwick on to the roof with so much precipitation as to impair the gravity of that gentleman's deportment very materially. 'Who—I? Brown paper parcel, here, that's all,—other luggage gone by water,—packing cases, nailed up—big as houses—heavy, heavy, damned heavy', replied the stranger, as he forced into his pocket as much as he could of the brown paper parcel, which presented most suspicious indications of containing one shirt and a handkerchief. 'Heads, heads— take care of your heads!' cried the loquacious stranger, as they came out under the low archway, which in those days formed the entrance to the coach yard. 'Terrible place—dangerous work—other day—five children— mother—tall lady, eating sandwiches—forgot the arch— crash—knock—children look round—mother's head off —sandwich in her hand—no mouth to put it into—head of a family off shocking, shocking!'

The Commodore coach is at present being rebuilt at the Doddington Carriage Museum, Chipping Sodbury. The original plates taken off it show it to be built by Thompson & Holland in 1839 and that it had subsequent overhauls by Holland & Holland. The coach was all urgency, refreshment breaks were kept to a minimum and you hurried over your meals as the following account will show:

'Twenty minutes allowed here, gentlemen, for dinner,' exclaims the coachman as we drive up to the Bull at Smallborough. What a scene of confusion ensued! Bells rang, ostlers hallowed, waiters ran or rather broke into that shambling shuffle whose secret seems to be known only to those who 'stand and wait'—at least no other creature practises it.

'Pleased to alight, ladies and gentlemen,' exclaims the landlord, addressing the four inside: while the ostler, bringing a somewhat crazy ladder, makes a similar request to the eleven outside.

The day has been a miserable specimen: incessant rain, with a biting easterly wind, giving an inappropriately jovial gentleman the opportunity of offering facetious remarks upon 'heavy wet' and 'cold without'. You enter the best parlour of the inn, anticipating a warm welcome and a share in their creature comforts looked forward to in such circumstances by all. But here the legal axiom that 'possession is nine points of the law', is realised to your horror and dismay in a sight of the first-comers on an earlier coach occupying every seat near the fire; a tablecloth covered with fragments, and a disarray of empty glasses tell a tale of another dinner having recently been 'polished off'. 'Waiter, waiter!' shriek half a dozen voices in as many keys, and in accents ranging from the imperious to the imploring. Enters then a slipshod being, with which watery eyes and apologetic mien. 'Here, you, wher's the dinner?' chorus the strange, half-drenched passengers. 'Dinner,'—scratching his head: 'er—well—er: beg pardon, gents, but the Independent was rather late today, and the Highflyer, she were down early, and —er—.' Well the gist of all these apologetics was that the company had to wait while the next joint was being dished up.

Meanwhile the Independents absorbing all the fire are bustled off by a portly man in a four-cornered hat and a huge taped box-coat, or 'upper Benjamin' as it used to be called. 'Gentlemen,' he roars, 'time's up.' With great to-do of cloaking, shawling, great coating, and paying they are outside, and we are, in the twinkling of an eye, in their fireside seats, listening to the curses levelled at the ostler by the outsides for letting the seats get wet. With a precautionary 'Sit tight' they lurch violently off, and we are left anxiously awaiting the arrival of that dinner.

At last it comes and procession of three—the landlady, parlourmaid and waiter—bearing dishes with ten covers. These battered relics removed a coarse fat leg of mutton, roasted to a cinder, is unveiled, together with a huge joint of boiled beef, very much underdone; potatoes, hot without and hard within and some gritty cabbage.

'Slice of mutton for a lady,' says the waiter approaching a stout gentleman in the act of helping himself to that part of the joint so highly prized by epicures, called the 'Pop's eye'. The direction of the knife is instantly changed, and the lady's plate filled with a somewhat less desirable ration. 'Please sir, a little fat', continues the assiduous waiter, 'and a little gravy'; he adds anxious to earn a tip from the old stager of the male sex, who invariably forwarded his demands, as coming from a lady. Numerous other applications are made to the carver, who disgusted with his place, helps himself to his coveted delicacy, and requests the waiter, with emphasis, to attend to the other passengers himself.

Time flies fast; and especially time devoted to pleasures, none of the party are aware how fast the glass has run, until the entrance of the coachman, informing all concerned that the coach is ready.

'Fully twenty minutes, sir,' replies that John.

'Abominable' continues the first speaker.

'Who riseth from a feast with that keen appetite that he sits down?' quotes a stage-struck attorney's clerk. 'I have,' mutters the Daniel Lambert of the party, 'and if Shakespeare quote that—well, coach dinners were not known in his time.' Now we do as we saw the Independents do before us, and fee the coachman, scramble for greatcoats, cloaks, shawls, umbrellas, in addition to ringing for the waiter to bring the brandy and water ordered ten minutes before but not yet forthcoming.

Halfcrowns and shillings are tendered in payment to the waiter, who of course has no change; what waiter ever had, when you were in a hurry? Now at the ultimate moment, the waiter appears with a tray containing 'one cold, without', 'four hots, with', 'two hots, sugar and no fruit', and 'three with the chill off'—the 'with' and 'without' referring to sugar, the 'no fruit' applying to lemon. Fortunate now are the owners of cold beverages, for none but a fire eater could swallow the scalding potations that are now left as perquisites to the waiter.

Amid the babel of departure may be distinguished 'Please remember the waiter, Sir!' 'Didn't take for your dinner, sir' 'Glass of brandy, ma'am' 'A basin of soup and a pint of ale gone away without paying!' 'Chambermaid, ma'am.' 'Ostler sir' 'I got you some nice dry straw.' 'Away, away.' 'Now, Gentleman, sit fast. Let 'em go. Jem I've got 'em!' and off goes the High Flyer. One gentleman however had matters organised and calmly drank his tea as the other passengers scrambled for their seats.

'You'll miss the coach, sir' shouted the landlord in his ear, under the impression that he was deaf and had not heard the stampeding feet.

' Want a spoon to stir my tea,' said the last remaining guest: 'Why didn't we have any?'

The landlord glanced hurriedly round—not one spoon of all those that had been on the table remained. He rushed out to the coach to find who among the passengers had stolen them; and by the time he had delayed the coach and everyone, the last passenger, having finished his breakfast at leisure, came out with the information that they had been found in the teapot, where, as will by now have been suspected, he had himself placed them.

A dinner generally left to the landlord consisted of eels, or other freshwater fish, dressed in a variety of ways, roast fowl, lamb or mutton cutlets, bread, cheese, and celery—charge 6s or 7s. If it took place after dark 2s or 2s 6d for wax lights.

For the good of the house and your certain discomfort a bottle of fine crusted port (probably two days in the bottle), 7s or a bottle of fine sherry just drawn from the wood, 6s. Waiter's fee 1s or 1s 6d per head. Breakfast with ham and eggs 3s, tea with a few slices of thin bread and butter was 1s 6d or 2s, a soda and brandy 1s 6d.

Of course there were good inns, but the general impression is that in the early years of coaching better establishments were few and far between, and another contemporary writer describes one of the less satisfactory inns in this way:

> Our passengers had been driven through the passage into
> a little, dark dingy room at the back of the house, with
> a dirty, rainbespattered window, looking against a white-
> washed wall. The table, which was covered with a thrice-
> used cloth, was set out with lumps of bread, knives, and
> two and three pronged forks laid alternately. Altogether
> it was anything but inviting, but the coach passengers
> are very complacent; and on the Dover road it matters
> little if they are or not. Coats No 1, No 2, and No 3 are
> taken off in succession, for some their silken jeopardy,
> hats are hid in corners. Inside passengers eye outside
> ones with suspicion... Presently the two dishes of pork,
> a couple of ducks, and a lump of half-raw, sadly mangled
> cold roast beef, 'What a beastly dinner!' exclaims an
> inside dandy in a sable-collared frock; 'the whole place
> reeks with onions and vulgarity.' 'No, harkee, waiter,
> there's the guard blowing his horn, and we have scarcely
> had a bite a piece,' cries Mr Jorrocks, as that functionary
> sounded his instrument most energetically in the pass-
> age; 'blow me tight if I stir.'

At the last halt passengers generally seized the opportunity
for a wash and brush up prior to arriving at their destination.
Highgate, Barnet and Hounslow were some of the famous
final stages before London. The smooth working of the stage
system depended greatly on the inns, which were fully or
partly owned by the coach proprietors. In the great years of
coaching, inns were efficiently run. The inn was no new
thing, the novelty lay in the proliferation of inns and the
drawing of them into a system. The inn sign is important,
because it links the landlord with the gentlemen. It is the
board itself that enobles the inn; we enter no mere drinking-
shop, but the house of a sort of gentleman. The coaching
inns functioned throughout twenty-four hours. The head

yard porter was an important man, whose duties covered the superintending of the horses, stables, coaches and harness. With tips he could earn in excess of £5 per week. Provincial inns improved over the years—much spurred on by competition. The guest invariably alighted at his inn and was welcomed at his room by a glass of choicest port or cordial. The Three Tuns at Durham was famous the whole length of the Great North Road for its glass of cherry brandy. Also well known was Mrs Botham of the Pelican at Speenhamland on the Bath road; an awesome figure dressed in black silk she always had ready a packet of brandy snaps for the children who travelled in the care of the guards.

A great many of our changes and habits in living, cheapening of food, alterations in the face of the country houses, towns and villages are due to the increased facilities of travel, which owing to the gradual improvements of our roads, the coaches and waggons were able to give us. Speech, clothing and local building styles were all so varied and different until quick travelling and conveyance of materials helped reduce all to one level. These were the days when Hounslow was known for timber-framed buildings, Hampshire and Wiltshire by chalk and flint, sandstone at Crewkerne and Chard and red sandstone and 'cob' in Devon. Survivals of these days are also the local delicacies. These obtained wider fame with coach passengers dining at country inns and were so appreciated that the passengers would take them home to relatives and friends. Stilton cheese, actually made at Wymondham in Leicestershire, was first discovered by a coach party who dined at the Bell at Stilton. The landlord obtained cheeses from Wymondham and did a roaring trade selling whole cheeses to the coaches to take away. The traveller would bring home many things which were not easily obtainable other than in the district of manufacture, and they became the spoils of travel—Scotch shortbread, Doncaster butterscotch, York hams, Grantham gingerbread, Banbury cake, Shrewsbury cakes, Bath buns, Cheddar cheese, Everton toffee, pork pies from Melton Mowbray, to name a few. These products showed the English tradition of hospitality and good cheer. Journeys were cold but hearts were warm. A typical change-over point on the main coaching road was Northallerton on the Great North Road, where the usual knot of sighteers would gather about the inns for the one event of the day, the arrival of the London coach. Among them one perceives 'the coachman wot is to take the next stage' out at elbows; three recruits with ribbons in their hats, not quite recovered from last night's drink, and stupidly wondering how the ribbons got there; and several errand boys wasting the master's time; and a horsey youth with small fortune but large expectations, who is the ostler of the place—the local man about town. In fact there was nothing else for the inhabitants of North-allerton to do for amusement but to watch the coaches, the post chaises and the chariots as they passed along the one long and empty street. At the height of coaching it boasted four coaching inns—the Black Bull, the King's Head, the Old Golden Lion and finally the New Golden Lion. As innkeeper, coach proprietor, and posting master, Frank Hirst exercised his business talents from the last-named inn for many years. At different times he horsed most of the principal coaches over his ground, which he held from Thormanby 15 miles south to Enter Common 8 miles north of his inn. It is, how-ever, somewhat unusual that the Golden Lion had a monopoly as a posting house in Northallerton whereas the mails were horsed from the Black Bull. Perhaps there was an agreement as to spheres of influence. Frank Hirst was a successful busi-nessman who died in 1835 a wealthy man.

The Golden Lion, as part of the Trust House Forte group, is still in existence. A Georgian building it had vast stables bordering a yard that ran a hundred yards back from the house. Its front rooms had deep window seats and small-paned windows. The old Assembly Room is still used, as are the post boys' quarters, although now modernised and turned into staff rooms. The old pump and stone water trough are also reminders of the past and in the hall stands a coaching clock. These clocks were found in many an old posting house and their origins are somewhat uncertain. They were of a distinctive type associated with inns. Their cases were nearly always plain, with a simple decoration on a black background, and varnished. Another one can still be seen working in the hall of the Crown Hotel and Posting House, Bawtry.

Frank Hirst horsed the Wellington from the Golden Lion which ran between London and Newcastle and changed horses here. At one time it was driven by Ralph Soulsey when running in competition on this road. So hard did he drive that on one occasion he succeeded in killing three of the four horses on the short 7-mile stage from Great Smeaton to Northallerton. Soulsey's third horse dropped dead outside the church and he brought the coach into the Golden Lion with a single horse. As railway competition drove the coaches off the road, the Wellington continued until at last it stood alone. One of the oldest coaches, it had beaten all the opposition until it became the last regular coach on this section of the Great North Road, but in the end it fell in the face of the common enemy—the railway. Passengers became scarcer until its last driver, Thomas Layfield, came out of Newcastle empty into Darlington, empty into Northallerton, empty into Thirsk and as its driver with bowed head drew up at each successive stage, the proprietors saw that the end had come, and the Wellington went off the road for ever.

Most half-timbered inns of any consequence had open galleries on two or three sides with the guest rooms leading off these galleries which were approached from the inn yard by outside staircases. As time went on these galleries were enclosed as protection from the weather. Around the inn yard were the loose boxes, the harness rooms and ostlers' rooms and above the stables in the larger inns were the post boys' quarters. There would be a mounting block for use by portly travellers and behind the inn yard a kitchen garden and bowling green, and again in the bigger inns a brew-house. The George, Huntingdon, is a living example of one of these inns. The Torrigdon diaries, *A Tour into Lincolnshire* (1791), records for Monday 20 June 1791:

> Growing tired I was glad to get to Huntingdon; which is eleven miles from Ramsey. At the George which is an old shabby inn, th' well stabled, I dined comfortably on beef steaks, peas, and gooseberry pie, with a pint of port; then walk'd thro' the town to the bridge, and returned over the castle hill: Huntingdon is a pleasant looking town; and the environs cheerful. I had to take tea at my return.

His bill for food at the George Inn, Huntingdon, was:

	s	d
Dinner	1	6
Wine	1	2
Fire		3
Tea		9
	3	8

It is a very old-established inn, having been in existence during the reign of Henry VIII (1507–47). In the coaching era it was one of the great posting houses on the Great North Road, and in 1839 the following coaches called there. It is apparent from the following extract that Huntingdon was well served:

Pigots Directory, September 1839
Inns. George Hotel Wm Hennesy, High Street. Coaches. All call at or go from the George Hotel, unless otherwise expressed.

TO LONDON the Royal Mail (from Edinburgh) every night at a quarter before eleven and the Royal Mail (from Louth) at a quarter before twelve—the Wellington (from Newcastle) every day at twelve ... all go through Royston and Hoddesdon.

TO LONDON, the Regent (from Stamford) every forenoon at eleven ... through Biggleswade, Baldock, Hatfield and Barnet.

TO BIRMINGHAM, the Rising Sun (from Cambridge) every morning (Sunday excepted) at a quarter past eight; goes through Thrapstone, Wellingborough, Northampton and Leamington.

TO BOSTON, the Royal Mail (from London) every morning at half-past two ... both go through Peterborough and Spalding.

TO CAMBRIDGE, the Blucher, every forenoon at eleven— the Alexander (from Leicester) every afternoon (Sunday excepted) at five—and the Rising Sun (from Birmingham) every evening at a quarter past six.

TO EDINBURGH, the Royal Mail (from London) every morning at half-past two, goes through Stamford, Newark, Doncaster, York, Durham, Newcastle, Berwick and Haddington.

TO LEICESTER, the Alexander (from Cambridge) every morning (Sunday excepted) at ten; goes through Stilton, Stamford, and Uppingham.

TO LOUTH, the Royal Mail (from London) every morning at half-past two, goes through Peterborough, Spalding and Boston.

TO NEWCASTLE-UPON-TYNE, the Wellington (from London) every night at ten, goes through Stamford, Newark, Tuxford, Doncaster and York.

TO STAMFORD, the Regent (from London) every afternoon (Sunday excepted) at four...

Another interesting inn still following the old traditions is the Crown Hotel and Posting House at Bawtry. The frontage is the same as it was in the coaching era and the colonnade leading from the archway is a vivid reminder of the bustle associated with the arrival or departure of the coaches. By the middle of the nineteenth century many seaside towns were advertising their claims as resorts but perhaps what is more interesting is a contemporary advertisement for the Royal 'Hotel' Southend. The hotel had arrived to become a facility to meet the needs of staying guests rather than an overnight halt during the course of a coach journey.

As, one by one, the coaches ceased running less inns were needed and whilst some continued the vast majority were used for other purposes. In cities and towns many were converted into shops and some became private houses; in the country districts many became farms, or again private houses. Of those which remained as inns a number of the larger establishments eventually became part of the present Trust House Forte group, which in its original format was started in 1903 by the 4th Earl Grey, as a bid to revive traditional English inn-keeping which was virtually destroyed by the railway age. (A list of some which are still in existence will be found in Appendix B.) This organisation has revived in Britain the term 'post houses' for its increasing number of motor hotels.

Page 143 (above) Lorna Doone coach at Horn's Cross, Devon; *(below)* Bude coach at the Hunter's Inn near Braunton, Devon

Page 144 *(above)* 'Comet' stage-coach in the snow at Doddington Hall; *(below)* London–Devonport (Quicksilver) Royal Mail passing Star & Garter Hotel, Kew Bridge, 1835

but not subject to naval discipline. Indeed they were liable to strike if they considered a boat unseaworthy. By the early nineteenth century it was realised that the office of inspector of packets appointed in 1790 was unfit to manage so large a fleet and in 1823 control of the Falmouth packets was transferred to the Admiralty.

Falmouth owes much of its prosperity to its establishment in 1688 as a Mail Packet Station. By 1827, the year after the Quicksilver Mail was established, there were thirty-nine vessels engaged in carrying seaborne mail from Falmouth to America, Brazil, the West Indies, Canada, Lisbon, Buenos Aires and the Mediterranean ports. Whilst the 'packets' were armed for defence they were forbidden to attack. Many mails of considerable importance were sent on by post boy if the regular mail coach had departed and it is recorded by F. Robbins in *Launceston Past and Present* (1888) that twenty of these special despatches passed through Launceston in one day.

At Exeter the contractor kept a horse and rider on day and night stand-by for this service and for heavier bags of mail sent by post chaise a team of four horses in harness was kept at constant readiness at the New London Inn, Exeter. The standing order was that the packets must put to sea immediately on receiving the mails whatever the wind, providing only that they could carry a double-reefed top sail—a striking proof of the certainty with which the good and well-founded sailing ship can clear the channel from Falmouth, and the Post Office agent, when giving evidence on the subject in 1840, could not remember one instance of such delay throughout his whole forty-five years of service.

In 1852 the service was transferred from Falmouth to Southampton and at the same time the gradual process of changeover from sail to steam was commenced.

If however the West Indian packets were short of coal they put into Falmouth; then omnibuses were hired and the mails sent to Plymouth in this way if the usual mail coach had left or was unable to convey the load. At Plymouth the mails were transferred to rail, for conveyance to London.

In the early days of the mail coaches many letters were sent 'privately by favour' on the extensive coastal shipping services which plied between many of our coastal ports at this time. Whilst such mail was conveyed in a clandestine manner for many years, it was enacted in 1799 that mail could proceed by private ships provided a ship letter levy was paid. In 1814 this levy was standardised at 8d. The advent of steam ships sailing in all weathers to regular schedules was a serious threat to the Post Office mail coaches and by the mid 1830s the Post Office decided it could benefit revenue-wise and at the same time offer additional facilities to the letter-writing public by operating postal despatches by coastal vessels at a rate equated to the prevailing ship letter rate of 8d. Although the inland postal revenue suffered, the move was on the promise that there would be an increase in the volume of mail going by the now reliable coastal steamers and that it was better to have a share of the traffic than suffer further losses.

The postage rates were:

up to 15 miles		4d (by inland post)
15 to 20	"	5d
20 to 30	"	6d
30 to 50	"	7d
50 to 80	"	8d
80 to 120	"	9d and so on

It will be seen that it was when there was a distance of 80 miles or more between seaports that the user saved money by opting to send his letter by coastal shipping. For instance London–Harwich cost 8d for 71 inland miles and the same by steamer, but London–Hull was 174 miles by road for 10d, Newcastle 280 miles 1s and Aberdeen 528 miles 1s 3d, whereas all were 8d by sea. The advantage to the user was limited by geographical considerations and the cost saving could be offset by the necessity of waiting the next departure of a ship and the time in transit.

The departure of the twenty-one mails from London was a popular and spectacular event with the coaches loading up at their respective inns at 7.30pm before proceeding to the Post Office yard to receive the mail bags at 8pm. There was an exception in respect of the Bath, Bristol, Devonport, Exeter, Gloucester, Southampton and Stroud which departed from the Gloucester coffee house, Piccadilly, at 8.30pm, the passengers being taken there by omnibus. The Post Office had been in Lombard Street, until the new General Post Office was opened in St Martins-le-Grand on 23 September 1829. The first to enter the gates as a result of intense competition had been the up Holyhead mail and last to depart the Dover mail.

All coaches were drawn by four horses except the Brighton, Portsmouth, Dover and Hastings, which were drawn by pair horses. This became one of the sights of the city—the punctual exodus of the mail fleet from the General Post Office at St Martins-le-Grand and a hundred passengers, thousands of letters and packages, the pick of the country's drivers erect on the box, the shine of the polished bodywork, the deafening rumble of wheels on the cobbles.

North country mails picked up their passengers at the Peacock Inn, Islington, immortalised in *Tom Brown's School Days*. Tom and his father had arrived in London from Berkshire by the Star, which put them down at the Belle Sauvage on Ludgate Hill. From there they went to the Peacock to pick up the Leicester Tally Ho! to Rugby at 3am. 'It don't wait for nobody' the 'Boots' at the Peacock warned Tom. Arrival at the Post Office commenced at 4.05pm and at varying intervals until all had arrived by 7pm. Sunday arrivals were variable as there was no Sunday delivery of letters and the coachmen used to meet at the various junctions for a 'good night out'.

Mails were conveyed by the packet boat service from Holyhead to Dublin, which was the centre of the postal service in Ireland. The Irish Post Office was separated from the British Post Office and had its own secretary and its two postmasters general. John Palmer did not therefore have anything to do with setting up the mail coach system in Ireland, this being done by a Scot named John Anderson. During the 1820s eight mail coaches departed from Dublin daily at 7pm. The most distinguished Irish coach contractor was an Italian immigrant, Charles Bianconi. He developed an extensive business conveying mails and passengers. Although other contractors sometimes employed two guards on each coach, Bianconi could boast in 1857 that in the forty-two years his coaches had been on the roads 'never has the slightest injury been done by the people to my property or that entrusted to my care'.

Lack of good roads was one of the main reasons why the mail coach service in Scotland was slow in spreading and before 1800 there was only one wholly Scottish service—that from Edinburgh to Aberdeen. However, the situation had much improved by the 1820s, developing concurrently with road improvements.

In 1834 the Post Office was paying hire charges of 2d per mile on forty-two mails, 1½d a mile on thirty-four and one 4d per mile. The Liverpool and Manchester conveyed the mailbags free and three paid the Post Office for the privilege. But the contractors were not happy about this and to enable them to earn increased revenue the rule that no more than three outside passengers may be conveyed was relaxed, and eventually many of the mails, like the stages, carried from eight to twelve outsides. But it was not the answer as the contractors preferred to concentrate on operating their own fast day coaches, which were more attractive to the public, who did not want the night travel irrespective of the extra seats. So the Post Office had to persuade the contractors to take on the mails by substantially increasing the rates. For Horne's 'Foreign Mail' carrying the 'black bags' (ie black tarpaulin to protect the mail from sea water) between London and Dover 1s 3¾d per double mile was paid; for the Carmarthen and Pembroke 8d; and 9d for the Norwich mail via Newmarket. The Chester originally rated at 1s and then went down to 3d but was subsequently increased to 6d resulting from passengers travelling on the direct Holyhead mail which itself increased to 6d per mile as a result of the fast day stages from Shrewsbury.

1837 was the last unbroken year of the mails starting from London and in 1838 there were fifty-nine four-horse units in England and Wales, sixteen in Scotland and twenty-nine in Ireland and in addition seventy pairs of horses. At this time substantial increases in speed took place and accidents were not uncommon. In February 1835 alone nine mail coaches overturned. Until 1838 an annual parade of mail coaches took place in London on the occasion of the king's birthday

Fig 7 General arrangement sketch-drawing of stage coach

and the king's health was toasted in porter outside St James's Palace.

Exeter then as now is the king pin of the road system in the West of England and by 1837 it had these mail coaches passing through: two for Falmouth, one for Devonport (the Quicksilver) but only one which terminated at Exeter—the New Exeter introduced in 1837. The Old Exeter, which continued on to Falmouth, was routed via Salisbury, Dorchester and Bridport, undertaking the journey to Exeter in twenty hours and to Falmouth in thirty-four and three-quarters. At one time the Old Exeter mail was nicknamed the Transport on account of the number of prisoners conveyed to Dorchester prison or to Plymouth for hard labour in the dockyard. The Quicksilver rerouted in 1837 via Salisbury, Amesbury and Ilminster instead of the previous route via Shaftsbury, Sherborne and Yeovil did the 176 miles between London and Exeter in 16hr 34min. It was the fastest long distance mail of them all with an average speed between London and Falmouth of $10\frac{1}{4}$mph, but having regard to halts for meals and Post Office business, certain stages must have been worked at 12mph. As the mail guard could order out post horses at the expense of the contractors if time was being lost, it meant that on occasions the coaches were hauled by six or eight horses.

In Falmouth the Royal Hotel was the terminal of the Royal Mail and Mr Newberry Cox, postmaster of Falmouth from 1856 to 1896, recalls that in 1842 as a boy:

He had been to Penrhyn and had reached Tehidy Terrace, when hearing the coach coming I whipped down on to the road and sprang on to the step of the coach, one hand holding on to the back of the guard's iron seat. Quick as thought the guard's foot jammed my hand, so that I was quite unable to move or get off the coach as I would gladly have done. The guard kept me there until we reached the Green Bank Hotel, when I was released, determined never to try that game again. I often laughed over the incident with Bryce (the guard) when he came under my official control in later years.

The last two horse mail coach services between **Falmouth**, Penrhyn, Helston, Marazion and Penzance and the last four horse mail between Falmouth and Plymouth ceased in 1863.

Palmer's plan provided that the mail guards should be employees of the Post Office but at first they were provided by the contractors who supplied the coachmen, horses and coaches. This proved unsatisfactory and after a short time the mail guards became employees of the Post Office and official superiors to the coachman. Generally retired soldiers, armed and uniformed, they soon became tyrants of the road. The country in general went in terror of them and their lethal weapons which the guard would fire at random during the journey.

The guards relying on the name of royalty, in the course of Irish road through North Wales committed great excesses. One, in a trifling quarrel, shot dead a poor old gate keeper... These guards shoot at dogs, hogs, sheep and poultry as they pass the road and even in towns to the great terror and danger of the inhabitants.

Of one accident in Ireland with firearms the report stated:

As the Sligo mail was preparing to start from Ballina, the guard, Samuel Middleton, was in the act of closing the lid of his arms chest, when, unfortunately, a blunderbuss exploded, one of the balls entered the side of a poor countryman named Terence Mc'Donagh, and caused his instant death.

During the wars with France the guards were offered a reward by the Post Office of £5 for every escaped prisoner of war killed or wounded—apparently it was not worth it to recapture them. This could not continue and in 1811 an Act of Parliament prohibited the firing of blunderbusses with a £5 fine for an offence. The blunderbuss was developed in the seventeenth century and although used in small numbers by the Austrian army it did not prove itself as a military weapon becoming, instead, a personal protection weapon. The spread of shot was from $\frac{1}{2}$in to 1in per foot and it was eventually realised that the trombone-shaped barrel had no effect on the spread. So that it could be carried in all weathers the barrel was made of brass and it could be loaded with a pound of buckshot and up to 160 grains of powder. It was a weapon to be loaded with care and only fired once.

The position of the mail guard had become desirable despite the poor salary of 10s 6d per week from which he had to pay to keep his equipment in order. Uniform of trousers, top boots, scarlet coat and gold-banded, black tall hat was provided free annually, but it was the perks which made the job worth while. A tip of 2s 6d from inside passengers and 2s from outsides was expected and guard and coachman divided all fares below 3s. A mail on the main roads could earn for the guard between £300 and £500 per annum in tips and payments from passengers and others for services rendered. The job appeared to have compensations besides salary and the verses about a 'mail guard now married written just before Waterloo' suggest this:

I've had many a hug at the sign of the Bear,
In the Sun courted morning and noon,
And when night put an end to my happiness there,
I'd a sweet little girl in the Moon.

Once guard to the Mail, I'm now guard to the fair,
But while my commissions's laid down,
Yet while the King's Arms I'm permitted to bear,
Like a Lion I'll fight for the crown.

Guards were involved in conveyance of the products of the activities of poachers, tea, meat and fish for villagers; purchase of wedding rings and conveyance of money for banking in London and legal documents. All this was unofficial but exemplifies the fact that they were very important persons. They conveyed news of great events and carried to the country the news of victory at Waterloo, with the coaches decked out with flags and laurel leaves. Cornwall was notorious for its 'rotten boroughs', so the final reading of the Reform Bill in 1832 was awaited with eager anticipations, so much so that at 4am on the morning of 7 June the reformers at Lostwithiel were awaiting the arrival of the coach, which was greeted by loud cheers and the town band. At Truro hundreds of people were there to witness the arrival of the coach, again with loud cheers, to which were added discharges of cannon to announce the news, to those who were not present at first hand. Popular media have developed to such a stage that in many instances we witness the news as it is happening, but have lost the excitement that must have gripped the gathering crowd as the time approached for the mail coach to arrive, first signalled with the sound of the guard blowing on his post horn—the 'old yard of tin'. These side-line activities resulted in Thomas Hasker being required to issue the following notice:

> In consequence of several of the mail guards having been detected in carrying meat and vegetables in the mail-box, to the amount of 150 pounds weight at a time, the superintendents are desired to take opportunities to meet the coaches in their district, at places where they are least expected, and to search the boxes, to remedy this evil, which is carried to too great a length. The superintendents will please to observe that Mr Hasker does not wish to be too hard on the guards. Such a thing as a joint of meat, or a couple of fowls, or anything or article for their own families in moderation, he does not wish

them from the privilage of carrying.

Stage coachmen and guards were not unaware of the lucrative sideline of conveying poachers' loot and in January 1820 a warning notice was inserted in *The Ipswich Journal*:

CAUTION: It having been strongly suspected that a great many stolen fowls and other stolen property have lately been taken up at different places on the London road, and conveyed by stage coaches and stage waggons, thus giving encouragement to a set of nightly robbers, who have lately been very active, by furnishing a ready opportunity of removing the fruits of their depredation, beyond the power of detection; the drivers of such waggons are desired to be extremely cautious as to what hampers or parcels, they may take up on the road, and especially in the night; and to refuse such as shall be tendered in a clandestine manner, or by suspicious characters. All drivers will be aware that they are responsible to the law should they presume knowingly to convey away stolen property.

On one occasion the guard of the Southampton mail was suspected of smuggling, and the customs officers attempted to stop and search the mail. But the guard threatened to shoot any man who attempted to search 'His Majesty's Royal Mail' and after the resultant row between the Customs and the Post Office the guard was warned but his conduct was approved.

The guard rode in the 'dicky' seat on the rear boot with his feet resting on the locker trap-door, which was the only means of access to the mail. In later years, however, the increase in the amount of mail required it to be conveyed on the roof as well. At first no 'outsides' were allowed but later one rode beside the driver, and two on a seat at the front end of the coach. Conveyance of another passenger on the roof was a £5 fine for the guard and any passenger permitted at the rear led to instant dismissal.

The main concern of the Post Office was, however, prevention of theft and although a mail coach was never robbed by a highwayman there were several instances of clever robberies, some of which are described in Chapter 9. Some guards were promoted to travelling inspectors of mail at a salary of £100 a year with 15s per day travelling expenses, but this was not likely to tempt many guards away from good-paying roads although the cross-country mails were not nearly so lucrative. The coming of the railways took away many of their perks and from 1842 mail guards received salaries ranging from £70 to £120 per year depending upon length of service. When the coaches finally ceased they were assured of continued employment as officials of the Post Office and many were employed at railway stations supervising the despatching of mails by train.

The outsiders are feeling the cold, feet stamping on the roof. Will any, at journey's end, be carried into the inn like boards, stiff as boards? Mr Bellaby is saying 'I will say this of the mail guards, that they are decent sober men and, though they sit upon guns, are rarely hot-headed enough to wish to use them'.

'There was,' says Mr Kirk, 'the case of the press-gang that stopped the Liverpool mail, saying there was a man had deserted aboard, and then the guard gave it them with his pistols.'

'It was,' you say gently, 'the Preston mail, though indeed it was outside Liverpool. And the guard merely threatened, no more. But the point was that there was trouble between the Postmaster General and the First Lord and the sailors were court-martialled.'

'Well that was right,' says Mr Bellaby. 'The mails must not be delayed. Is there not a fine of fifty pounds for that?'

'I wonder, though,' says Mr Jeffers, 'that the guards of the mail coaches are as loyal as they are. Considering not just the bad pay but also the niggardliness of the Post Office in giving recognition or rewards for service beyond ordinary duty.'

'There is one thing and one thing only they must attend to,' says Mr Bellaby, 'and that is the delivery of the mails. The mails must get through. Under no matter what difficulties.'

'Very well,' says Mr Jeffers, 'but what of this Chester mail guard who worked four hours in water up to his waist, when the road flooded—Sweatman I believe his name was, and a name highly appropriate—rescuing passengers and saving the mail and then everything froze. It was the passengers got him that reward of ten shillings, but then a shilling was deducted because the mails were late. What do you think of that? And that other guard, I forget his name, who walked seventy miles with the mail bags when the coach broke down at Cirencester. Seventy miles through ice and snow. His great reward was five shillings more on week's wages. I could tell you many stories.'

You could tell many stories too. The guard died after pushing the mails in a cart through snow drifts. The Dundee mail that had to be dug out of snow nine times in one journey. And that shocking winter of '31 when the Dumfries–Edinburgh mail got stuck. What were the names of the two men now?

'You will mind,' says Mr Jeffers, 'that time of the Dumfries–Edinburgh mail being buried deep, and the rule that the passengers must fend for themselves, the passengers were left there to freeze. But MacGeorge the guard said he and the driver—Goodfellow I believe his name was—must ride horseback with the mails, and so they did. But then the horses could go no further. So the men walked, as best they could. Then the next day a shepherd saw a bright flash on the hill, so went forth

to see. What should it be but the brass plate of one of
the mailbags, tied safe to a post. And then, days and days
later, the bodies of the two were dug out. Now I cannot
vouch for this, but the shepherd swore there was a kind
of smile of satisfaction on the face of MacGeorge.' A
pause to do silent homage to the memory of MacGeorge.
And, you remember the time when the fog was so thick
that the coachman could not see the rumps of his horses,
and the mail got through; the time when the Gloucester
and Stroud mails collided in a pea-souper, but the mails
got through. Fog according to the Postmaster General,
did not exist; fog was no excuse for not delivering the
mails. The mails must always get through.

'But,' says Mr Bellaby, 'the mails have not always got
through. The times, thank God, are freer than they were
from footpads and the like, but the mail-bags have been
snatched at Wetherby not long ago. Many roads,' he ex-
plains to Mrs Tate, 'meet at Wetherby. It is roughly
midway between Edinburgh and London.'

'The Angel,' you say, 'perhaps the best inn of them all.
A hundred horses stabled there, and four public dining-
rooms.'

'It was at Wetherby,' says Mr Bellaby, 'that men in
cloaks and masks rode into the Post Office itself and
grabbed the sacks from the very hands of the Postmaster.
Yes, [he says to you] I know the Angel well.'

Young Henry starts to laugh. 'Why are you laughing?'
asks his mother. 'It is about the guard who mistook the
mail-bag in the dark for the horse's nose-bag. And it was
the nose-bag that got through.' It is a good story enough;
the adults laugh too, though not so loud as Master Henry.

'Well,' says Mrs Tate, 'We shall soon be coming to our
ten-minute rest. I shall be glad to stretch my limbs and
have something hot. I warrant you gentlemen will also.'

'Yes, indeed,' Master Tate says; 'I could eat something.
I could eat ten million jam tarts covered with buckets
of custard.' A strong stomached boy. As for your own

stomach, it is not bearing up too well. The reek of the coach is in no wise mitigated by the winter air, for your travelling companions will not let much in. As for your bones, they are racked. You will be glad of that ten-minute break from the glories of coach travel.

Every guard had a list of twenty-six instructions for carrying out his duties and the following was printed and distributed in November 1829.

GENERAL POST OFFICE

Mail Guards

1. The guard is intrusted with the care of the letter bags, and he is to be answerable at his peril for the security, safe conduct, and delivery of them sealed.

2. He is not to quit or desert the mail or bags of letters, or suffer any loitering or unnecessary stopping at public houses, or other misspending of time, upon the road, or neglect to give information of such misconduct on the part of the coachman; if he does, he will be liable to be taken before a justice of the peace, and committed to hard labour and imprisonment for one month, and he is subject to all other punishments and penalties which the law (as specified in the several Acts of Parliament relative to the Post Office) have hitherto inflicted upon post riders who have neglected their duty.

3. If in post towns, he, on any account, collects or delivers letters or packets, or does so upon the road, (except in some particular cases where the postmaster of the district or superior officers are authorised to order it) he will be liable to an information before a justice of the peace, and to the payment of ten shillings for every letter; agreeable to an Act of Parliament passed in the first year of the reign of His Majesty George the Third, and will be dismissed the service.

4. The guard is to behave with civility to passengers, to assist the coachman on any occasions that are

consistent with his situation as protector of the mails, and do not take him out of sight of the place where they are deposited.

5.   He is on no account whatever to give up his station to another person. He is to take care that his fire arms are kept in clean and good condition: that they are always loaded and primed when on duty, and on no account whatever to be wantonly discharging his blunder-buss or pistol as the carriage is going along the road or through a town; for every such offence he forfeits two guineas, agreeable to an Act of Parliament; he is also to draw the charge of this as soon as he has ended his journey.

6.   He is to sound his horn as a signal for carriages to turn out of the way upon the approach of the mail coach; also to warn turnpike men of its coming, that no unnecessary delay may be occasioned, and likewise to prepare postmasters against its arrival, and horsekeepers to bring out their horses at each of the changing places; and he is to sound it always as a signal to passengers when the time is expired that is allowed in the time bill for their stopping to refresh, and to use his utmost exertions to prevent delay in all cases whatever.

7.   It is the guard's duty to see the time bill is justly dated and signed at every place, and where he cannot obtain the postmaster's date and signature, to do it correctly himself, to insert the number of passengers travelling by the coach, for which a space is provided, and to deliver it carefully to the guard who succeeds him at the end of his journey, or to the postmaster at the place where the route of the mail coach ends.

8.   He must be very careful of the time piece and time bill, and if either at any time should be broken, torn, or lost, immediate notice must be given at this office, or the cause communicated to the post master of the nearest place that he may report the same.

9.   Guards will be suspended and otherwise pun-

ished, who neglect to deliver the bye bags properly, which for want of better attention have been frequently carried beyond their distance, and sometimes even brought up to London.

10. Drunkenness, or disobedience of official orders, will be punished with dismissal.

11. The guard is to prevent, if possible, any more passengers being conveyed than the contract allows, and if a guard neglects to give immediate notice of any violation of this article, with an account of the parties who are necessary to it, it will be considered as a very material breach of his duty, and he will be punished accordingly.

12. It is a very necessary part of his duty to report the earliest intelligence of all accidents, delays, or obstructions, of inattention or want of readiness in horsekeepers, of misconduct in any of the parties concerned in the performance of the duty, and of all occurrences whatever, that have a tendency to impede the progress of the mail coach, or may in any respect be proper to be communicated. He will, if a mail coach breaks down, describe what particular part broke on his bill, and the next day, as soon as possible, by letter give information how it happened and what damage was done.

13. If the mail coach breaks down on its way to London, and it cannot be repaired in half an hour, or in such time that the mail may arrive at the Post Office by the proper time, the guard is to ride on with it by horse or chaise; the postmasters and contractors have directions to furnish such chaise or horse which the Postmaster General will pay for the use of. The guard must do all his business at the different offices, and his road business, and take care that he performs his journey in the same time as if the coach travelled.

14. If the mail coach should fail between stage and stage, the guard is to press one of the mail coach horses, and ride on to the next stage with it.

K

15. If in travelling from London an accident happens, he is to use all proper expedition in repairing the coach, and if it cannot be done in an hour or an hour and a half, as the circumstances of that particular road will allow the guard must take chaise to forward the mail.

16. Guards are on no account to carry parcels, whether for private use or for sale; and are to permit mail coach contractors or postmasters to examine their mail box, and see their time bill.

17. It is the guard's duty to report if horses are unfit for the service; if the harness or reins are bad.

18. It is the guard's duty always to have a bag of tools complete; and every week when they go to receive their wages, the postmaster has orders to examine their fire arms, to see if they are perfectly clean-barrel, lock, and every part that they have a blunderbuss and case, a pair of pistols and holsters, a powder horn, bullet mould, screw driver, touch hole picker, and lock for the mail box likewise the several articles enumerated* and also a double or long spreading bar; and if they do not produce them clean and in the most perfect repair, they will not be paid and the postmaster will report such negligence to this office.

19. In case of any accident that occasions the coach to be stopped in its progress, it must be the guard's duty to see that the contractors provide horses for removing it to its proper place as soon as possible; or in the case of the contractor's refusal, the guards are to get horses elsewhere, and send an immediate account of the same to this office.

20. The mail box, which in the regular coaches is

---

*2 trace chains, 1 pole chain, 2 tug chains, 1 hatchet, 1 strong hammer, 1 wrench hammer, 1 small wrench, 1 small saw, 1 drift pin, 1 large spike bit, 2 gimlets, 1 main bar, shackles, bolts, clips, nuts, worms, screws, nails, cord.

calculated for the reception of letter bags, and such things as only relate to the conveyance of the mail, must be confined entirely to that use, and neither packets, parcels, luggage or any other description of thing whatever, must be put therein.

21. No luggage can be allowed on the roof which interferes with the proper packing and safety of any sacks of letters which the mails are in some cases obliged to carry there. No luggage to be placed on the roof till after the boot is full, and then only that which belongs to passengers. No more than three articles, being portmanteaus or carpet bags, are, on any pretence, to be allowed whether they be large or small; and the largest portmanteau is not to exceed 2 feet 4 inches in length, and 1 foot 6 inches in height. They are never to be placed on each other. By portmanteau is meant, any article made of or covered with hair, and of course all boxes of other materials, bundles, baskets etc, are to be rejected. The portmanteaus are to be fastened at one end of the seat irons, and a staple will be placed on each side of the coach, for one strap to go over and further secure them.

22. The guards are never to allow an extra passenger to be put inside, except with the full consent of all the other passengers. Nor must any person, of any description whatever, not being an inspector of the mail coach department be suffered to ride with the guard upon the mail box, unless in order to further some necessary business belonging to the service, an authority to justify the same is issued from this office, with the office seal affixed to it.

23. It is like wise the guard's duty constantly to examine the condition and state of the mail coaches, particularly of such spare coach or coaches as stand upon any part of the ground they work, and to see that they are properly cleaned and taken care of; and to report any deficiencies or imperfections in them; and each guard is to be accountable for whatever damage the coaches may

sustain that are under his care, and also for the loss of all seats, lamps, windows or articles of any kind.

24.   If at any time the coaches are not provided with the best lamps and lights, the guards must report the same.

25.   They must never leave their mail box unlocked when the mail is therein, or take their lock off where the guards are changed, till the succeeding guard has put his lock thereon.

By command of the Postmaster General
CHARLES JOHNSON
Surveyor and Superintendent

Timekeeping was of utmost importance and to this end mail guards were supplied with an official time piece (clock) sealed in a wooden case; of particular interest is that the clocks were regulated to lose or gain so many minutes in twenty-four hours in order to accord with local time. Hasker's advice to one guard reprimanded for running late on account of passengers being delayed at their dinner was:

Stick to your time bill, and never mind what the passengers say respecting waiting over time. Is it not the fault of the landlord to keep them so long? Some day, when you have waited a considerable time (suppose five or eight minutes longer than is allowed on the bill) drive away and leave them behind. Only take care you have witness that you called them out two or three times. Then let them get forward how they can.

The guards checked their timekeeping by reference to the milestones and their time bills were carefully examined at the Post Office and contractors who failed in their time-keeping would receive the following circular from Hasker:

I am commanded by the Postmasters General to inform

you that the time lost on your ground between —— and —— by the mail coach, as it was on its way to — was — minutes: and I am further directed to desire you will immediately give such orders that time may be kept, for it is only to such as keep time, and do their duty well, the additional mileage can be given.

Contractors who failed to take heed were threatened with loss of contracts although this does not seem to have been effected on many occasions. The time bill was in reality a log sheet on which had to be written any details of accidents or any unusual occurrence which might occur on the journey. Hasker was much concerned with public complaints regarding incivility. The previously mentioned increase in rates did not solve the problem of rates and the arrival on the scene of the railways must have come as a great relief to the Post Office who transferred the mails to the Liverpool & Manchester Railway from the opening in 1830. By an Act of Parliament passed on 14 August 1838, by which the conveyance of mails by railways was authorised, the Post Office was ready to take advantage of the opening of the London & Birmingham Railway in September 1838. As railways pushed further out of London the mails were transferred to them, the coaches meeting the trains at railheads. The London & Southampton Railway, for instance, opened to Woking on 23 May 1838, thence to Winchfield and on 10 June 1839 reached Basingstoke, which became the terminal of the West Country mails, although the coaches of the Exeter Telegraph and Quicksilver (Devonport mail) were brought down by train and horsed onwards from Basingstoke. These shortenings were accompanied by advertisements similar to the following which appeared in *The Times* during October 1838:

Bagshot–Surrey 49 Horses and Harness. To coach proprietors, Mail contractors, Post Masters and others—To be sold by Auction, Mr Robinson, on the premises Kings Arms, Inn, Bagshot, on Friday, November 2nd. 1838 at twelve o'clock precisely, by order of Mr Scarborough, in consequence of the coaches going per Railway.

About forty superior good sized, strongly, short-legged, quick actioned fresh horses and six sets of four-horse harness, which have been worked the 'Exeter Telegraph', Southampton and Gosport fast coaches and stage one of the Devonport Mail. The above genuine stock merits the particular attention of all persons requiring known good horses, which are for unreserved sale, entirely on account of the coaches being removed from the Road to the Railway.

2 May 1840 saw the coaches cease between London and

Fig 8 General arrangement sketch-drawing of Cornish horse bus

York; in 1842 the York to Newcastle-on-Tyne mail coaches ceased and on 5 July 1847 they departed from the Newcastle-on-Tyne to Edinburgh road. One of the last to go was the Derby to Manchester in October 1858 and finally the last of all, on 1 August 1874, that between Wick and Thurso.

And so it all came to an end and the sentiments of the time are best summed up by an old coachman:

Them as 'ave seen coaches afore mails came into fashion 'ave seen something worth rememberin'! Them was 'appy days for old England, afore reform and rails turned every-thing upside down, and men rode, as nature intended they should, on pikes [turnpikes], with coaches and smart active cattle and not by machines like bags of cotton and hardware.

CHAPTER NINE

PASSENGERS, HIGHWAYMEN AND ACCIDENTS

THERE IS much humour in coaching: the fat passenger was always a favourite, and a story is told of a corpulent man who was accustomed to book two seats. On one occasion his scheme was noted by two companions, who decided to play a trick by booking seats which they occupied by facing one another. Although politely requested to change they refused despite the explanations of the fat man, who determined to get his revenge. At the next stage he persuaded a chimney sweep to ride on the coach at his expense. The sweep caused great annoyance to the two companions, who asked the fat man at the next stage how far the sweep would be travelling. He replied:

I took two seats so that, although corpulent, I should annoy no one. You prevented me occupying them, therefore I filled the remaining seat with Chummy, and he goes as far as the end of my journey. But I will dismiss him if you will agree to what I proposes. When I engaged him, I agreed to 'pay him for his time' and to pay his fare home. With all other expenses incurred. He is now at breakfast. If you agree to pay him, he goes no further; if not, he proceeds.

Having listened to this ultimatum and being completely discomforted, they accepted these terms, and the sweep was dismissed.

It is interesting to note the change in ladies' fashion during the coaching era of 1750–1850. During the first fifty years the most fashionable dress was the crinoline and train, complete with high wigs, plumes and large hats. The crinoline was supported by a series of oval hoops giving the lady width and of necessity requiring a wide pathway to walk on. The spectacle of a lady being settled into a coach was quite an occasion, in fact one wonders if indeed it was possible for four ladies to travel inside the same coach together at all. However by the turn of the century the Regency influence was beginning to take over and dresses became much more simple, with long, straight, clinging lines, much more suited to the now popular vogue of travelling. Still fashion is always contrary and by 1835, with the Victorian age just around the corner, wide dresses with more elaborate trimmings were returning to the scene. One wonders if perhaps it was with relief that the fashionable ladies witnessed the arrival of the railway carriage obviously much more suited to cater for their whims and fancies in fashions.

Every passenger who travelled by coach took with him his road book, which gave details of coaches, routes, toll gates, packet boats, inns, mileages, market days and populations. In 1764 it is recorded that the *Traveller's Aid* directed that a traveller was required to take on his journey the following essential items:

A portfolio case of instruments for writing
A sketch book and a note book
An opera glass
A tinder box
A night lamp
Sheets and a quilt
A mariner's compass in a snuff box
A thermometer and a tooth pick in a cane
A barometer in a sword
A blunderbuss and a case of pistols

HIGHWAYMEN

In the old days no traveller going north along the Great North Road left Alconbury without first priming his pistols. The passengers by mail and stage put their watches and jewellery secretly between their skin and underclothes, for at Alconbury Hill was the threshold of a robbing place only second to Gads Hill near Rochester, Hounslow Heath and Finchley Common. It was called Stonegate Hole, between the sixty-fourth and sixty-fifth milestones from London. These highwaymen were always armed and consequently very courageous. Stonegate was a deep solitary hollow at the foot of a northward slope shut in by dense woods—an ideal spot. In the later coaching era when the road was lowered and earth filled into the hollow, many bones were found during the course of this work and were supposed relics of unfortunate travellers, who had met their death by the highwaymen. Such was the reputation of the place that the tale is told of an ostler, who, after helping change horses, would short-cut across the fields, come upon the coach and collect many valuables, simply by levelling a tin candlestick at the coachman, guard and passengers.

Throughout the coaching era, highwaymen, highway robbery of post boys, stage coaches, post chaises and all sorts and conditions of wayfarers became commonplaces of travel. The

100 GUINEAS
REWARD.

GENERAL POST-OFFICE,
16th July, 1827.

WHEREAS on the Night of Thursday the 12th Instant, about a Quarter-past Ten o'Clock, the Driver with the Mail between Leatherhead and Dorking, was feloniously stopped by two Men on the King's Highway, between Leatherhead and Dorking, opposite Givon's Grove, when the Men fired two Pistols at the Driver, and severely wounded him.

The Men are stated to have been dressed in dark Clothes.

WHOEVER will come forward and give such information as may lead to the apprehension and conviction of the Offenders, shall receive a Reward of

One Hundred
GUINEAS.

A Ramrod was found near the spot, and is supposed to have dropped from the Pistol of one of the Offenders.

If either of the Persons concerned in the said Felonious Attack, or any Person knowing thereof will surrender himself, and make discovery whereby the other Offender or Offenders may be apprehended and brought to justice, such Discoverer will be entitled to the said Reward, and will also receive His Majesty's most gracious Pardon.

BY COMMAND,

FRANCIS FREELING,
SECRETARY.

Printed by S. Bennett, Whitefriars-street, Fleet-street,
In His Majesty's Stationery office.

Fig 9 Offer of reward for apprehension of highwaymen
(see pages 177-8)

peak period for highwaymen was between 1650 and 1750. They were most common in the seventeenth century and had largely died out by the eighteenth century. They came from all backgrounds and many followed honest trades as 'covers' during their criminal careers. Highwaymen were not just poor men, often being the dissolute sons of the aristocracy, faced with drinking and gaming debts. Oxford was a notorious place for highwaymen—with its impoverished university students. Some of the highborn highwaymen were able to use their influence to escape the gallows and it was written by Francis Jackson that 'He can't be hanged who hath five hundred pounds at his command'. However, they were still about in the early nineteenth century and in Wiltshire between 1806 and 1824 six highwaymen were hanged at Fisherton gaol, Salisbury. Dick Turpin was the prominent hero of romance, but innumerable other practitioners surpassed him. Claude Du Vall, who robbed and danced on Hounslow Heath; Abbershaw, the terror of the Surrey Commons; Captain Hind, soldier and gentleman, warring with authority; Boulter, whose depredations were conducted all over the country; the Golden Farmer on the Exeter Road— all those and very many more were infinitely superior to Turpin and, as they phrased it, 'spoke to the coaches with great success during their brief but crowded careers'. Travellers considered it inevitable to be robbed once on a journey, but soon found that the profession of highwayman was an overcrowded one and were often robbed a number of times on one journey. In fact the highwaymen would even practise on one another. One of the worst places in Yorkshire for highwaymen and footpads was the Calder Valley, the narrow pass between Todmorden and Hebden Bridge surrounded by steep, dark cliffs offering plenty of shelter for footpads and robbers to descend at great speed on unlucky travellers. Robbery was so common that by the mid eighteenth century, people were advised to tear banknotes in half when sending them through the post, dispatching each half separately to reduce the attraction to thieves. Penalties for a captured highwayman were as barbaric as suited the temper of the age: he was hanged in public and his carcase strung from a gibbet for all to see slowly rotting away.

Masked men, usually coarse and abusive, were both a nuisance and a menace to life on the roads. Tyburn continued to take toll of them and wayside gibbets to creak with their carcases on windy nights. Another grim relic is Caxton Gibbet, near Cambridge, rising dark and forbidding against the translucent evening sky. Does the troubled ghost of Young Gatward, gibbeted here for robbing the post boy on this lonely spot, ever revisit the scene we wonder? The end to the problem came as a result of the Act of Limitations of Cash Payments, passed in 1797. After this, travellers began to carry less money on their journeys, but serious robberies continued, particularly of goods of high value in small compass.

Turnpike Trusts at this time encouraged sabbatarian feeling by charging double fees on Sundays, in the full knowledge that travellers risked prosecution under the Sunday Trading Act, which for many years prevented coaches running on Sundays. Consequently highwaymen did not work on Sundays but when at last the mail coaches started to run seven days a week and the Post Office set an example of Sunday travel, away went the highwaymen's day off and again they plied their trade.

Horace Walpole, writing from personal experience of an evening in 1781, expressed the view that 'unless country squires would take time off from shooting partridges and shoot highwaymen instead society would be dissolved':

Lady Browne and I were, as usual, going to the Duchess of Montrose at seven o'clock. The evening was very dark. In the close land under her park-pale and within two yard of the gate, a black figure on horseback pushed by between the chaise and the hedge on my side. I suspected it was a highwayman, and so, I found, did Lady Browne...I heard a voice cry 'Stop!' and the figure came back to the chaise. I had the presence of mind before I let down the glass, to take out my watch and stuff it within my waistcoat, under my arm. He said, 'Your purses and watches.' I replied, 'I have no watch.' 'Then your purse.' I gave it him; it had nine guineas. It was so dark I could not see his head but I felt him take it. He then asked for Lady Browne's purse, and said 'Don't be frightened; I will not hurt you.' I said 'No; you won't frighten the lady?' He replied, 'No; I give you my word I will do you no hurt.' Lady Browne gave him her purse and was going to add her watch, but he said, 'I am obliged to you, I wish you goodnight,' pulled off his hat and rode away. 'Well,' said I, 'Lady Browne, you will not be afraid of being robbed another time, for you see there is nothing in it.' 'Oh, but I am,' she said 'and now I am in terror lest he should return, for I have given him a purse with only bad money that I carry on purpose.' 'He certainly will not open it directly,' said I, 'and at worst he can only await for us at return; but I will send my servant back for a horse and a blunderbuss.' Which I did.

Highwaymen about to be hanged were accompanied on their cart journey to the gallows by Chaplins or Ordinaries, in general a bunch of debauched and corrupt men, who derived a large part of their income from the sale to local printers of concocted last words of convicted felons. Their literary efforts sold like 'hot-cakes', as for example:

The last Speech, Confession and dying words of James Andrew, who was executed in the Grassmarket of Edinburgh, upon Wednesday the 4th day of February 1784 for the horrid crime of Highway Robbery.

I James Andrew, though but a young man in age, must acknowledge to my shame, that I have too early been introduced into the paths of vice. I was born of honest parents, nigh to the city of Belfast in the Kingdom of Ireland and put to apprentice to a linen weaver in that place, I served out my time, and happy had it been for me that I continued at my trade in innocence and in my native country. But no sooner was I free of my indentures than a roving inclination to see Scotland with the accounts in our country that the wages were better than at home. I determined to go over, and made my way to this country where I got employment at my business and might have lived happily thereat. But being too early set at liberty and the world before me, I was soon perverted into the bewitching sins of drunkeness and whoring, which led me into the extremes of vice; folly and dissipation, made me a Sabbath breaker, a drunkard, rake and a fool. About this time I fell in with...at Dalkeith, she has born me two children, but family disputes prevents me from saying further about them, than the connexion was unlucky for me, and being thus circumstanced, I enlisted for a soldier in the South Fencible Regiment, where I behaved tolerably well as a soldier, and was freed from the clamours of a wife. I dare not say that this way of life did me any good, for in the public towns, such raw foolish youths as I, were soon brought into the company of bauds, whores and jilts. All of which put me on the disagreeable and unhappy schemes of seducing young women to supply my extravagances. Among others I seduced a servant girl in Queensferry, to steal seven guineas from her master to get married with me, and the poor girl was publicly disgraced for it, and the money in my pocket all squandered in drink.

I did not at that time consider the very bad consequences that might attend this way of life, nor the unhappiness of what might follow. I went from Sin to Sin, gloried in wickedness and followed the courses of

vice, when the Regiment was reduced, I was so habitu-
ated to idleness and drunkeness that I could not settle
at my trade, and having my wife at Dalkeith, and the
other from Queensferry still looking to me for justice.
I was obliged to enlist in the 61st to keep myself from
being harassed by the clamours of women I had injured.
The Supporting of such courses, wasted my money and
obliged me to fall upon desperate shifts: by which means
I came to rob David Dykes of his watch and money, as
libelled against me.

Indeed I cannot help throwing blame upon some of
my acquaintances or companions, who led me into the
desolate way of life and engaged me in scenes, which has
brought me to this disgraceful end, to avoid the clamour
of women, I enlisted in the sixty first Regiment of foot,
and though all was over but my desolate conduct having
occasioned new demands, I went with Hay and Patterson
to the place where we met with John Dykes at the end of
the meadow, or hope park, where we robbed him of a
silver watch, which was found on me, and proved the
means of my being convicted. The young woman ob-
served the blood upon our hands as a favourite of Hays
who wished to make all things clear, but it would not do,
the evidence was strong against me, although the other
two did the deed, and Hay having friends and connections in the country, was slipped out of the Tolbooth in
a manner I cannot prove, therefore I'll say no more of it.
I was bred a Roman Catholic, am not twenty two years of
age, I have been much obliged to Mr Bell, for introducing me in the principles of christianity.

And now as a dying man, I forgive judges and jury and
pray to God that all involuntary faults may be forgiven,
as I hope for forgiveness myself, through the merits of a
Saviour.

For though others were deeper concerned in the crime
than I, they were undoubtedly in the line of their duty,
and condemned me according to the laws of the country.

I have been a drunkard, a sabbath breaker, disobedient to my parents, and guilty of many faults attendant upon vice, but my trust is in the Lord of hosts, to cleanse me from all presumptuous sin, and make me appear as spotless through the merits of my divine Redeemer. Who can understand his errors, I am sent off a sacrifice to the laws of my country in the prime of youth, not yet twenty years of age, though young in years, may the Lord of all grace, mercy and peace, make me ripe for the inheritance of the blessed, and let all foolish youths take warning from me to avoid the paths that lead to death and destruction. Into thy hands O Lord Jesus I commit my departing soul and die an unworthy member of the Holy Catholic Church.

JAMES ANDREW

There was rank if not honour amongst these thieves and the highest order were the pickpockets, then the highwaymen, and finally the worst of all thieves and rogues, the footpads who were on foot and often murdered for the sake of a few shillings.

The mail coaches were however immune from attacks (although mail carts did not escape the highwaymen's attention) and the Post Office introduced enactments dealing very severely with highway robbery applied to mail coaches.

100 GUINEAS REWARD

General Post Office
16th July, 1827

Whereas on the Night of Thursday the 12th Instant, about a Quarter-past Ten o'clock, the Driver with the Mail between Leatherhead and Dorking, was feloniously stopped by two Men on the King's Highway, between Leatherhead and Dorking, opposite Givon's Grove, when the Men fired two Pistols at the Driver, and severely wounded him. The men stated to have been dressed in

L

dark Clothes. Whoever will come forward and give such information as may lead to the apprehension and conviction of the Offenders, shall receive a Reward of

ONE HUNDRED GUINEAS

A Ramrod was found near the spot, and is supposed to have dropped from the Pistol of one of the Offenders.

If either of the Persons concerned in the said Felonious Attack, or any person knowing thereof, will surrender himself, and make discovery whereby the other Offender or Offenders may be apprehended and brought to justice, such Discoveror will be entitled to the said Reward, and will also receive His Majesty's most gracious Pardon.

BY COMMAND,

FRANCIS FREELING,
SECRETARY.

The standard reward for arresting an highwayman was £200 in the case of an attack on the mail, with another £100 if within 5 miles of London. The occasional robbery of the mails did take place but never with violence. In February 1810 a lock was wrenched off the hind boot of one of the mails, while the guard was away and sixteen north country bags were stolen. These robberies became so frequent that in January 1813, the superintendent of mails was forced to issue the following notice:

The guards are desired by Mr Hasker to be particularly attentive to their mail box. Depredations are committed every night on some stage coaches by stealing parcels. I shall relate a few, which I trust will make you circumspect. The Bristol mail coach has been robbed within a week of the banker's parcel value £1,000 or upwards. The Bristol mail coach was robbed of money in the 3rd instant to a large amount. The Expedition coach has been twice robbed in the last week—the last time of all the parcels out of the seats. The Telegraph was robbed last Monday night between the Saracen's Head, Aldgate and Whitechapel Church, of all the parcels out of the dicky. It was broken open while the guard was on it, standing up blowing his horn. The York mail was robbed of parcels out of the seats to a large amount.

Despite the warning small thefts still occurred. Then in 1822 came the classic instance—the robbery from the Ipswich Mail, when notes worth £31,198 mysteriously disappeared. A month later the bulk of them (£28,000) was recovered, only £3,000 successfully disappeared. The need for the Carriers Act 1830 described in Chapter 4 was spelled out very clearly. The closing great robbery of the coaching age was of £5,000 in notes from the Potter (Manchester and Stafford) coach in October 1839.

Adventures, says the proverb, are to the adventurous, but in coaching times they befell the quiet traveller as well as the adventurer. Such was the startling adventure on the night of 20 October 1816. The up Exeter Mail left Salisbury with what it thought was a large calf trotting beside the horses. When the coachman pulled up at the lonely inn at Winterslow Hut (later the Pheasant Inn) the horses were very agitated and nervous and as one of the team was suddenly seized by the supposed calf, the terrified team began to kick and plunge. The guard promptly drew his blunderbuss and was about to shoot, when several men arrived on the scene and it appeared the ferocious calf was actually a lioness escaped from a travelling menagerie. A large mastiff was used to decoy the lioness who, leaving the horses, seized the dog and tore it to shreds. Eventually the lioness was recaptured and taken back to captivity. The leading horse Pomegranate was badly mangled but survived and was sold and exhibited by the showman with much financial success coming the way of the menagerie.

Just outside Andover the Quicksilver mail had an accident when the shaft of a waggon coming down Abbots Hill ran into the off wheeler which was killed outright. Driver and guard were thrown over the coach on to the dead wheeler, but they quickly recovered and reharnessed the other three horses 'pick axe' (ie one leader only) and drove on to the end of the stage at Winterslow Hut.

Dark nights in wild, lonely country gave rise to many strange experiences, aided, doubtless, by the potency of the parting glass as by the blackness of night and rugged country. Harper, in his book *Coaching Days of Yore*, relates a not unusual incident.

> The adventures of Jack Creery and Joe Lord, coachman and guard of the pair horse Lancaster and Kirkby Stephen mail, one snowy night, from a case in point. They had the coach to themselves for it was not good travelling weather. Creery we are told 'felt sleepy'—a pretty way of saying he was intoxicated—and so the guard took the reins. His condition was only a shade better than his companion, thus they wandered in the snow into a by-lane between Kirkby Stephen and Kirkby Lonsdale, and so lost his way. After floundering about for some time, he aroused and their united efforts, after alighting many times to read signposts, brought them in the middle of the night to a village, where they were found by the aroused villagers, loudly knocking at the church door, under the impression that it was an inn. That snowstorm must have been a particularly blinding one, or the brandy at their last house of call, unusually strong.

Severe weather in the shape of frosts, thunderstorms or gales was powerless to stop the coach service, but exceptionally heavy snowfalls, and floods often brought individual coaches to grief. In the severe winter of 1798–9 when snow fell heavily and continually at the end of January and during the first week of February several mails, missing on 1 February, were still being sought on 27 April. By May day, however, they all succeeded in running again. In 1806, another exceptional winter, Nevill a guard on the Bristol mail was frozen to death.

However, the worst coaching winter was undoubtedly that of 1836–7. Snow started falling on (Sunday) Christmas Day 1836. Incidentally in this country where heavy falls of snow are quite rare, exactly half a century later Christmas night 1886 (also a Sunday) was marked by a well-remembered snowstorm which disorganised the railway service as effectively as that of 1836 did the coaches and broke down nearly every telegraph pole and wire in the country. The snowstorm of 1836 affected the whole country and only on two mail routes were communications kept open. Fourteen mail coaches were abandoned, and as the snowstorm continued for nearly a week many more ceased running. The two routes remaining open were those to Portsmouth and Poole. Why this was so is not entirely known, the coachmen and guards were very strong men but then most of the men engaged on the mails were very strong men. The roads were also very exposed in places, and bleak. Never before in recollection had the London mails been stopped for a whole night only a few miles from London and never before had the link between London and the South Coast been stopped for two whole days. In succession accompanying high winds had the effect of driving the snow drifts up to 20ft high and in places higher. The extraordinary and almost unprecedented snowstorm put an almost complete stop to the transaction of business in many parts of the country and the regularity of the mail and stage coaches was completely disorganised. The snow commenced with a north-east wind, which veered round to almost every point of the compass. Near Chatham the snow was 30–40ft deep and everywhere it was higher than the roofs of the coaches. The depth of snow had the effect of obscuring the natural features of the country; thus when the last snowed-up mails were recovered many were found to have strayed from their routes. At Haughley, near Bury St Edmunds, the mail was stopped where the snow was stated to have drifted to a depth of 40ft. Further south conditions were a little better and the London–Ipswich mails both up and down were conveyed by forwarding the mails by men on horseback or in post chaises. Typical of the difficulties experienced occurred on 29 December when the Yarmouth mail was despatched on horseback to Lowestoft and from there by coach and six horse to Yoxford. Here the leg of the near wheeler got over the pole and broke the futchings and the mail proceeded towards Ipswich in a post chaise with four horses.

Herculean efforts were made to clear the roads and during the course of Saturday 31 December all the mails at last arrived in London. The Edinburgh mails were last to arrive at 8pm, having come by post chaise and four horses from Newcastle. Indeed none of the North Country coaches had been able to proceed further south than Newcastle. The guards all described the cold as beyond anything they had previously experienced. Four coaches were abandoned between Nottingham and Mansfield and the sixteen passengers were taken to a small cottage. Fortunately the cottagers had recently killed a pig so there was plenty of meat but there was little bread or other foodstuffs and no prospect of obtaining any. At midnight on the Friday a mail guard was sent from London on the Dart steamer with instructions to leave mail bags at Margate and Ramsgate where he should also leave the Dover mail bags for onward conveyance by land, proceeding afterwards to Calais. The weather was so bad the captain could not put in at Margate and with only the greatest skill was able to enter Ramsgate when, due to the severity of the weather, he refused to sail for Calais.

One of the most famous guards was Moses James Noble who ended his career in 1891 as superintendent of the mails at Paddington railway station. Born in 1817 at Norwich he worked on several of the mail coaches finishing up in 1838 as guard on the Cheltenham–Aberystwyth mail until it came off in 1854. He then became travelling inspector to the Post Office on the Great Western Railway between Paddington and Exeter. One of his experiences illustrates the very difficult conditions under which the men could on occasion be expected to work:

We had left Gloucester, he said, and all went on pretty well until we came to Radnor Forest, where we got caught in such a snow storm that it was impossible to take the coach any further so we left it. I took the mail bags and with the assistance of two shepherds made my way over the mountains. It took us five hours to get to the other side, to an inn at Llandewy. There we met the up guard, Cordery, who took my guides back again. It was not many hours before the abandoned coach was completely covered with snow and there it remained buried for a week. Well, Cordery it seems had fallen down in the snow from exhaustion and had to be carried by the two shepherds to the 'Forest' inn, on the other side of the mountain, where he remained for some days to recover. I had to proceed with my bags, so I got a chaise and pair from Pen-y-Bont and another at Rhayader, but was unable to take that very far owing to the snow. There was nothing for it but to press on again on foot, which I did for many miles, until I came to Llangerrig. There I found it was hopeless to think of going over Plinlimmon and was informed that nothing had crossed all day; so I made up my mind to go round by way of Llandidloes, and a night of it I had, I was almost tired out and benumbed with cold, which brought drowsiness, I found it very hard to resist. If I had yielded for one instant I should not be telling these tales now. When I got about eight miles from Aberystwyth I found myself becoming thoroughly exhausted, so I hired a cart for the rest of the journey and fell fast asleep as soon as I got into it. On arriving I was still fast asleep, and had to be carried to bed and a doctor sent for, who rubbed me for hours, before he could get my blood into circulation again. I had then been exposed to that terrible weather for fifty hours. Next day I felt a good deal better, and started back for Gloucester, but had great difficulty in getting over the mountain. I had the honour of receiving a letter from the Postmaster General complimenting me on my zeal and energy in getting the mail over the mountains. Even when there was no snow, the wind on the top of Plinlimmon was almost more than we could contend with. Once indeed, it was so strong it blew the coach completely over against a rock; but we soon got that right again, and always afterwards took precaution of opening both the doors and tying them back, so that the wind might pass through the coach.

Mail coach guards were required to enter up details of delay resulting from snow in a special book as follows:

GENERAL POST OFFICE
December 1830.

SNOW BOOK

In this book the guard will carefully fill up the columns, either when the leaders are used for the mails, or chaises, or saddle horses are taken in this winter on account of snow.

The duty of the guard, is always to keep the mail coach going in its regular manner, unless he sees the necessity of assistance to prevent great loss of time. It will be the particular duty of the guard, to make a good arrival in London. When the time can tolerably be kept with leaders, it is the proper mode to take them, and never to have a chaise, unless the coach, with its whole load, cannot travel at all.

The guard is still to mark on the time bills in the usual manner when horses are had, and is to keep the book the better to enable Mr Johnson to check the bills when

received. A copy of the book, twice a week, is to be sent to
Mr Johnson

Date	From what place	To what place	No of miles	By whom supplied and whether leaders or otherwise	Reason	By guard's order or not	For guard's signature remarks

The snowstorms however produced many happy parties
arranged by the passengers at their enforced overnight stays.
They would gather round the hearths drinking jorums of
punch and telling dramatic stories. Marooned in a village on
the Great North Road, one party was in the Green Man inn
and another in the Dun Cow. Among the coaches were the
Manchester Beehive and the Red Rover. On the morning of
their enforced leisure the coachman, guard, and passengers
made up a poaching party with two guns amongst the group
of sixteen; Jack Goodwin, guard of the Beehive, was the only
fortunate one—he shot a hare. In the evening a dancing party
was held. Next day Goodwin became wandering minstrel with
a party down the Rugby Road who were royally entertained
at the farmhouses with elderberry wine and pork pies. After
another pleasant evening of conviviality they were off again
to London.

Floods were far more dangerous than snowstorms and the
Great North Road between Newark-on-Trent and Scarthing
Moor was particularly susceptible. The Trent flooded at the
slightest provocation, covering many miles with water. On
these occasions the outsides fared better because whilst they
clung to their seats the insides were in constant terror of
drowning and often stood on their seats for safety.

In August 1829 when most of Scotland was devastated by
extraordinary floods a stirring episode occurred in connection
with the mails running through Banff. The tradition that His
Majesty's mails were to be stopped for nobody and hindered
by nothing on the road was all very fine, but often it was

pushed to absurd lengths. During the preceding days the Inverness mail had diverted from the Banff route owing to floods but to the amazement of the locals the following mail arrived within minutes of its scheduled arrival time. After much dissuasion by the locals the mail set off to cross the bridge over the River Dovern. The furious current caught the coach on the road down to the bridge and swept it into Gillan's Inn, where the desperately struggling horses were thrown off their legs. A boat was put out to try to free them but only one of the four survived. By this time the guard was clinging to the roof and the coachman was hanging on to a lamp-post, regretting too late the official ardour and slavery to tradition which had wrought such havoc. After they and the mail bags were rescued they were not allowed to depart without much Aberdonian plain speaking on their folly. Luckily there were no passengers on this occasion, but one assumes they would still have proceeded without giving them further consideration.

On 11 September 1829 the Birmingham and Liverpool mail suffered an unfortunate accident owing to flood at Smallwood Bridge near Church Lawton where the road was crossed by the River Weaver. Unknown to the mail the flooded stream had burst the arch of the bridge so when the coach came to the spot the axles were deep in water, and it fell into the hole and was overturned. Of the three inside passengers, one escaped. He was a young man who broke the window and quickly climbed out. The horses were all drowned, the coachman fortunately was washed against a tree stump, and although nearly stunned he hung on until he was saved. The guard was saved in a similar manner. Accidents of a similar nature were a frequent occurrence and the rigours of coach travel were such that a seasoned traveller said 'Give me collision, a broken axle and a overturn, a runaway team, a drunken coachman, snowstorms, howling tempests; but Heaven preserve us from floods!'

Racing for wagers, the pleasure of amateur coachmen or an endeavour to obtain business in a highly competitive trade, resulted in many accidents and the *Leeds Mercury*, referring to 'another of those alarming accidents to which stage coach passengers are so much exposed', gave this account:

It appears that about six o'clock in the morning ... both the coaches from Leeds to York entered the town at full gallop and the True Briton, in attempting to pass the other coach, ran over a basket of dung which stood in its way, and was overturned. At the time when the incident happened, the coach had six inside and four outside passengers; but though the position of all the passengers was perilous in the extreme, only one lady received any material hurt. The lady who was one of the inside passengers, finding that the coach was likely to upset, seized hold of the door, and the coach falling upon her hand, either crushed off all her fingers, or bruised them so terribly, so as to render amputation necessary.

Another contest between two Greenwich coaches in April 1815 racing from Westminster Bridge became so frightening to the passengers that some of them endeavoured to jump off and whilst one escaped with only a few bruises, another 'fell on his face against the gravel with such force that his nose was flattened; his forehead was cut in a most dreadful manner, as were also his hands and knees'.

Some of the cargoes the waggoners conveyed were extremely dangerous, particularly gunpowder. This was illustrated during 1776, when a waggon on passing through Brick Hill, Northamptonshire,

was set on fire by the friction of the axle-tree, and three barrels of gunpowder among the loading took fire, by which the goods were blown up in the air, and totally destroyed to the amount of one thousand pounds.

A few years later the same thing happened to a waggon loaded with gunpowder as it entered the village of Talk-on-the-Hill, Staffordshire. One account of the mishap mentioned that the explosion

> shook the whole village and scattered the limbs of the horses and driver to a great distance, one horse, with the driver, was forced through the wall of a house, which fell upon the inhabitants, some of whom were bruised, in a shocking manner. The whole village is little better than a heap of ruins.

Another explosion happened on the waggon belonging to Betts & Bury of Ipswich, whilst returning from London one day in August 1819. The top of the waggon was found to be on fire, and the flames soon spread to the load of gunpowder. 'The whole load was blown up', reported the local newspaper, 'and scarcely an article of any description saved.' A similar fate had befallen Hearne's Stowmarket waggon in August 1815, when it was reported that

> the road for a considerable space, and the neighbouring fields, were covered with various property, half consumed, or otherwise destroyed, consisting of soldiers' accoutrements, wool, hops, a quantity of books, chests of tea, etc and the remains of the waggon.

One of the great objections used by the coachmen against the railways was their danger. In fact to add emphasis to this, the day the Liverpool & Manchester Railway opened (15 September 1830) a prominent politician (Mr Huskisson) was run over by the first train. There was a favourite saying among coachmen: 'In a coach accident there you are; in a railway accident where are you?'—thus trying to prove that coach accidents were a mere trifle compared with railway accidents. However, there were many tragic coaching accidents quite apart from those caused by weather, particularly the drowsy folk on the box seats who quietly fell off and broke their necks without any public notice being taken. Some of the accidents are described below:

1819: Coburg coach upset on the up journey at Cuckfield. The horses fresh and dashing away collided with a waggon. All eleven outsiders were injured; one died the next day.

1826: The Leeds & Wakefield True Blue galloping down Bell Hill on the wrong side collided with a coal cart. The coachman died instantly and two passengers died later.

April 1826: One of the more serious accidents befell the London & Dorking stage at Ewell, the coachman, Joseph Walker, who was also the proprietor, alighted and carrying no guard left the reins to a boy sitting on the box. The boy cracked the whip and the horses set off at full speed. They dashed down an awkwardly curving road by the church and into a line of wooden pailings which were torn down for twelve yards. The coach was upset and all the passengers were hurled from the roof and one unfortunate woman fell on some spiked railings and was dreadfully mutilated beyond recognition and died a lingering death in great agony. The grave stone of this lady is still to be seen in Ewell churchyard inscribed—'Catherine, wife of James Bailey, who in consequence of the overturning of the Dorking coach April 1826, met with her death in the 22nd year of her age.'

30 October 1832: Brighton mail upset at Reigate, coachman killed on the spot. The three outsiders suffered fractured ribs and minor injuries.

June 1837: The Lincoln and London mails came into collision at Lower Codicote near Biggleswade. The driver of the up mail, Thomas Crouch, was partially drunk at the time and owing to his wanderings and a curve in the road he did not see the approach of the other mail. The coachman made room for him but still they collided violently. The coach driven by Crouch was turned completely round and ran twenty to thirty yards in the opposite direction and finally settled in a ditch. Crouch was injured and died later. The passengers were only slightly injured but two horses were killed.

September 1838: The Edinburgh & Perth Coburg was loading passengers and luggage at Newhall's Pier, South Queensferry, when the leader horse suddenly turned and the coach and horses disappeared over the quay wall. The outsiders saved themselves by jumping off. One was thrown far out to sea, but fortunately was able to swim and came ashore safely. Two passengers inside were drowned. Nine years later on 16 February 1847 a similar accident happened to the Torrington & Bideford Omnibus when the horses took fright and plunged with the vehicle into the river from Bideford Quay. Of the twelve passengers, ten were drowned.

The railway journals which quickly came into existence noticed the increasing number of coaching accidents, the *Railway Times* reporting twenty in a few weeks. The last years of coaching did in fact see far more accidents than the old days. Many of the coachmen who in all weathers had driven for many years over well-known routes met their death in unforeseen manner. One instance of this was coachman William Upfold—unlucky Upfold who was coachman of the Brighton & Southampton Times. He was fifty-four and had been a reliable coachman for thirty-five years but had a series of accidents from 1831 onwards. In that year he received two broken legs and in 1832, trying to stop his horses, he was kicked and fell under the wheels, and one leg was again broken. He eventually recovered and in 1840 for some unexplainable reason he pulled the wrong rein at Salvington corner and toppled the coach over with the result that all the passengers were injured and Upfold died from his injuries. By 1840 however the railway accidents were becoming more common and the coaching ones were forgotten with the past so that artists of the time were inspired to paint pictures like *Road versus Rail* showing a smart coach bowling safely along with smug passengers watching a railway accident.

One of the later incidents which occurred is worthy of note. Charles Ward, a fine old coachman, kept going in Cornwall after coaching had ceased in the rest of England and tells the story that befell the Bath & Devonport mail. An outside passenger, Mrs Cox, an 'immense woman' who kept a fish stall in Devonport Market, was being handed a glass of something warm by the ostler of the inn at Yealmpton. The horses, being left unattended and hearing movements on the coach, thought (for it was said that coach horses actually did think) that it was their coachman, started off and trotted without their driver at their ordinary speed the whole seven miles to the door of the Kings Arms at Plymouth where they usually stopped. Mrs Cox terrified to scream for fear of startling them merely waved frantically to attract attention. The horses however skilfully avoided everything on the road and also crossed Laira Bridge and through the toll bar. The two passengers inside were in ignorance of the whole affair until the coachman and guard arrived in haste in a post chaise. It was said that it took many quarterns of gin to steady the nerves of Mrs Cox and the incident became the chief landmark of her career. A similar incident befell a mail coach at Bude during a change of horses. When the fresh team had just been harnessed, they started off for Bodmin without coachman, guard or passengers, who were left standing. The other horse which had just been taken out followed, galloping behind the coach.

CHAPTER TEN

THE END OF THE ROAD

DURING THE period 1823–38 steam-powered carriages were tried and indeed used on some roads. There were several engineers interested but most noteworthy were Sir Goldsworthy Gurney and Walter Hancock. Gurney first tried a steam carriage on the road in 1827 and, during a trial run to Melksham with a steam tractor on 28 July 1829, was caught up in a hostile demonstration during which the tractor and Gurney's party were stoned with quite serious results. Gurney entered into an agreement with interested persons to introduce his steam carriages on a franchise basis on routes from London to the West of England, Manchester, Liverpool, Brighton, Southampton, Birmingham and Holyhead at 6d per mile hire or outright purchase at £1,000 each. The first trial in public service came during the early part of 1831 between Cheltenham and Gloucester. It was successful and might well have gone from strength to strength, had not the Turnpike

Trusts involved increased their tolls for steam carriages to a prohibitive level and even, it is alleged, obstructed the roads with stone and gravel with the result that one vehicle suffered a broken axle. Although there were seven important steam-carriage companies in existence between 1832 and 1838 the actions of the Turnpike Trusts ensured that steam carriages were commercially impossible to operate. By way of example a coach between Liverpool and Prescot paid 4s whereas a toll of £2 8s was imposed on a steam carriage.

Hancock's steam carriages were at least as efficient as Gurney's and after experimenting for four years he proposed in 1828 a service between London and Brighton and although it did the journey in 1832 no service was started. Hancock commenced in 1833 with steam buses between Paddington and the City and had a number of successful long distance journeys to his credit but for the same reasons as Gurney was unable to enter them into regular public services. It is interesting to speculate on the effect these vehicles might have had on road traffic and indeed the development of the railway network had they been officially encouraged. When Sir Rowland Hill in 1840 introduced the penny postage this greatly increased the mail to be conveyed and had railways not been constructed so rapidly, there must have been great difficulty and increased expense in conveying the mails, as it would have been impossible for the mail coaches to carry them and passengers as well.

In the early days of railways, even after the Liverpool & Manchester Railway, public opinion, and indeed to a large extent official railway opinion, was that the railway would handle freight, but the coaches would continue for passengers. Lovers of the road declared they would never go by rail, but when some urgent occasion arose, demanding speed, they went by train and by and large became converted. As passengers transferred to rail some coaches were immediately withdrawn, others endeavoured to continue, reducing costs in the

M

SWAN WITH TWO NECKS, LAD LANE,
GENERAL COACH OFFICE.

The following ROYAL MAILS

Leave the above Office every Evening at a Quarter-past Seven; on Sundays at Seven o'Clock.

BATH and EXETER ROYAL MAIL, through Devizes, Melksham, Wells, Bridgewater, Taunton, and Collumpton.
BIRMINGHAM ROYAL MAIL, through Stony Stratford, Daventry, and Coventry.
BRISTOL ROYAL MAIL, through Reading, Newbury, Malboro', Calne, and Chippenham.
CAMBRIDGE ROYAL MAIL, through Buntingford, Royston, and Melbourne.
CARLISLE and EDINBURGH ROYAL MAIL, through Chorley, Preston, and Garstang.
CHESTER ROYAL MAIL, through Salop, Ellesmere, & Wrexham.
DEVONPORT ROYAL MAIL, through Chudleigh and Ashburton.
EXETER ROYAL MAIL, through Salisbury, Sherborne, Yeovil, Crewkerne, and Honiton.
HOLYHEAD ROYAL MAIL, through Stony Stratford, Towcester, Daventry, Dunchurch, Coventry, Birmingham, Wolverhampton, Shiffnall, Shrewsbury, Oswestry, Langollen, Corwen, and Bangor.
HULL and LINCOLN ROYAL MAIL, through Peterborough and Sleaford.

KIDDERMINSTER ROYAL MAIL, through Birmingham, Dudley, and Stourbridge.
LIVERPOOL ROYAL MAIL, through Dunchurch, Coleshill, Lichfield, Newcastle, and Warrington.
LYNN and WELLS ROYAL MAIL, through Ely and Downham.
MANCHESTER ROYAL MAIL, thro' Northampton, Harborough, Leicester, Derby, Ashbourn, Leek, and Macclesfield.
MILFORD HAVEN ROYAL MAIL, through Cardiff, Swansea, Carmarthen, and Haverfordwest.
NORTH DEVON and BARNSTAPLE MAIL, through Bampton, and South Molton.
NORWICH ROYAL MAIL, through Chelmsford, Colchester, and Ipswich.
PLYMOUTH and FALMOUTH ROYAL MAIL.
STROUD ROYAL MAIL, thro' Abingdon, Farringdon, Cirencester, and Chalford.
SOUTHAMPTON and POOLE ROYAL MAIL, through Farnham, Alton, Alresford, and Winchester.
SCARBORO' ROYAL MAIL, thro' Beverly, Driffield & Bridlington.

POST COACHES

MORNING

	Time.
ABERYSTWITH, through Leominster	quarter before 5
BIRMINGHAM, (Tantivy) through Oxford	7
BIRMINGHAM, (Tally Ho!) in 11 hours, thro' Stony Stratford	7
BLANDFORD, (Herald) thro' Basingstoke & Salisbury, half-past	8
BRISTOL and BATH, (Emerald) without Fees, through Devizes and Melksham	
BRISTOL and BATH, (Cooper's) Old Company's Coach, through Calne and Chippenham, without Fees to Coachmen and Guard	7
BRIGHTON, through Ritstead	7
CANTERBURY, through Faversham	quarter before 10
CANTERBURY	quarter before 8
CARMARTHEN, through Aberygavenny	quarter before 5
CHELTENHAM, through Wycomb & Oxford, quart. bef.	8
CHESTER, through Birmingham	7
COVENTRY	7
DARLINGTON, (Highflyer) through York	quarter before 5
DEAL, through Sandwich	8
DERBY, (Times) through Loughborough	quarter before 7
DORCHESTER, (Highflyer) thro' Stamford & Grantham, quart, bef.	8
DORCHESTER, (Herald) thro' Sutton Scotney & Salisbury half-p.	8
DOVOR	quarter before 8 and quarter before 10
DUDLEY	quarter before 7
DURHAM, (Highflyer) thro' Retford & Ferrybridge	quarter before 5
EDINBURGH, through York	5
EXETER, (Herald) through Blandford, and Dorchester	half-past 8
FALMOUTH, (Herald) only one Night out, through Launceston, Bodmin, and Truro	8
GLOUCESTER, (Retaliator) through Northleach	quarter before 8
HOLYHEAD, (Tally Ho!) through Shrewsbury	7
LEAMINGTON	7
LEICESTER, (Times) through Harboro'	quarter before 7
LEICESTER, (Red Rover) thro' Northampton & Welford, ½ past	10
LIVERPOOL, (Tally Ho!) through Birmingham	7
LIVERPOOL, (Red Rover) through Welford, Ashby-de-la-Zouch, Uttoxeter, Burslem, and Hanley	half-past 10
MANCHESTER, (Tally Ho!) thro' Birmingham, with preference to sleep at Birmingham, or proceed at pleasure	7
MARGATE, through Canterbury	quarter before 8
NEWBURY, (Esquire) through Wokingham, and Aldermaston	10
NEWCASTLE, (Highflyer) through Thirsk, Northallerton, and Rushford	quarter before 5
NORWICH, (Times) through Bury and Scole	half-past 9
NOTTINGHAM, (Times) through Northampton	quarter before 7
OXFORD, through High Wycomb	quarter before 9
OXFORD, (Royal William) through Uxbridge	12
PARIS, by way of Dovor	quarter before 8
PARIS, by way of Dovor	quarter before 10
PLYMOUTH, (Herald) thro' Blandford and Honiton	half-past 8
PORTSMOUTH, through Godalming	9
RAMSGATE, through Rochester	8
READING, (Zephyr) through Windsor and Bracknell	10
SALISBURY, through Basingstoke and Stockbridge	half-past 8
STAMFORD, (Highflyer) thro' Baldock & Wansford, quarter before	5
SOUTHAMPTON and LYMINGTON (Independent) quarter-past	8
WORCESTER, through Tewksbury	quarter before 8
WARWICK, through Coventry	7
WEYMOUTH, (Herald) thro' Salisbury & Dorchester, half-past	8

MORNING continued

	Time.
WINDSOR and ETON	quarter before 8
YORK, (Highflyer) through Newark & Doncaster, quarter before	5

AFTERNOON

	Time.
BRIGHTON	3
BRIGHTON	4
BATH, (Age) through Newbury and Melksham	half-past 3
BIRMINGHAM, (Greyhound) thro' Stony Stratford in 11 hours	half-past 4
BIRMINGHAM, (Erin-go-Bragh) through Woodstock	half-past 4
BRISTOL, (Age) through Marlborough and Devizes	half-past 3
BRISTOL and BATH, (Cooper's) Old Company's Coach, through Devizes and Melksham	half-past 4
CAMBRIDGE, (Rocket) thro' Ware, Buntingford, and Royston	3
CANTERBURY, (Tally Ho!) through Ospringe	half-past 4
CANTERBURY	6
CARLISLE, (Defiance) through Preston	half-past 6
CARLISLE, (Royal Bruce) through Garstang	quarter before 8
CHESTER, (Greyhound) through Birmingham	half-past 4
COVENTRY, (Greyhound) through Dunstable	half-past 4
DERBY, (Defiance) through Leicester	half-past 6
DERBY, (Royal Bruce) through Northampton	quarter before 8
DOVOR	6
DUDLEY, (Greyhound) through Coventry	half-past 4
EDINBURGH, (Defiance) through Carlisle	half-past 6
EDINBURGH, (Bruce) through Carlisle	quarter before 8
GLASGOW, (Defiance) thro' Kendal and Dumfries	half-past 6
GLASGOW, (Bruce) thro' Kendal and Dumfries	quarter before 8
HOLYHEAD, (Greyhound) through Shrewsbury	half-past 4
IPSWICH, through Colchester	quarter before 5
LEAMINGTON	5
LEICESTER, (Defiance) through Northampton	half-past 6
LEICESTER, (Bruce) through Harborough	quarter before 8
LIVERPOOL, (Tartar) thro' Leamington & Warwick quart. before	5
MANCHESTER, (Defiance) thro' Leek & Macclesfield, half-past	6
MANCHESTER, (Bruce) through Derby, Belper, Matlock, Bakewell, and Buxton	quarter before 8
MILFORD HAVEN, (Age) through Swansea	half-past 3
NOTTINGHAM, (Commercial) through Northampton and Leicester	quarter before 8
NOTTINGHAM, (Defiance) through Leicester	half-past 6
NOTTINGHAM, (Bruce) through Loughborough, quarter before	8
OXFORD, through Henly	half-past 4
PARIS, through Amiens and Chantilly	7
PORTSMOUTH, through Godalming and Guildford	6
PORTSMOUTH, through Petersfield	6
SHREWSBURY, (Greyhound) thro' Birmingham	half-past 7
SOUTHAMPTON, (Royal William) through Farnham, Alton, Alresford, and Winchester	4
SOUTHAMPTON, (Quicksilver) through Basingstoke and Winchester	6
STAFFORD, through Wolverhampton and Penkridge, half-past	6
SWANSEA, through Bristol and Cardiff	half-past 3
TAUNTON, through Cross and Bridgewater	half-past 3 and 6
TENBY, through Newport and Carmarthen	half-past 3 and 6
WARWICK, (Tartar) through Southam	quarter before 5
WINDSOR and ETON	5

Parcels and Luggage conveyed Daily to all parts of the North, and to every City and Manufacturing Town in the Kingdom.
The Public are respectfully informed, that every information relative to the Steam Packets connected with the above Coaches, may be obtained at the Swan with
Two Necks; Spread Eagle, Gracechurch Street; and Spread Eagle Office, Regent Circus, Piccadilly.

Passengers and Parcels are regularly booked at the Spread Eagle Office, Regent Circus, Piccadilly, and Angel Inn, St. Clement's Strand, and conveyed by all the above Coaches. Goods received for the Monarch, James Watt, and Soho Steam Packets, for Edinbro', Glasgow, Paisley, & all Parts of Scotland, every Saturday till 6 o'Clock.—WILLIAM CHAPLIN & Co.

Ilsine, Printer, 38, Gracechurch Street.

Fig 10 Coaches from William Chaplin's, Swan with Two Necks, Lad Lane

face of declining revenue. First a reduction from four to three horses and then to a pair and coach, which obviously became slower than hitherto which made the railway even more attractive to the last remaining faithful coach travellers. The standards of comfort declined and coachman and guard (if retained) with the coach presented a seedy and uncared-for appearance. No ostlers or stablemen remained and the coachman had to see to his horses as best he could until in the end there were no travellers and the coach made its final journey down the road and into oblivion.

Despite newspaper comments that the railways were inefficient and railway officials insolent, attempts to revive coaches on certain routes were unsuccessful. It seems that many coach proprietors were deceived by newspaper reports, which they believed represented public opinion, which it was alleged wanted a stage coach revival; but they ought to have known better. Transport is first judged in terms of time taken on the journey and on this score they could not beat the railways, so many coach proprietors lost a large amount of money. Sherman was one of the diehards who was misled and he attempted to revive the London–Manchester Red Rover in association with John Wetherald & Co of Manchester but failed. Some of the obscure cross-country routes continued to survive until the beginning of the twentieth century when they were replaced by the new coach—the motor bus and, of course, the motor car. Most of the coaches were broken up but a number of mail coaches were sold and shipped to Spain running for many years on roads from Malaga in the south, to Victoria and Salamanca in the north.

The British custom of keeping to the left makes good sense when viewed from the coachman's seat. The whip hand had to be free both to control the horses and to cut at on-coming teams, which threatened to block the way. The ordinances of the postmaster general designed to expedite the mails and keep them safe did much to establish the traffic laws of today

TIME-BILL, LONDON, EXETER AND DEVONPORT ("QUICKSILVER") MAIL, 1837.

Contractors' Names.	Number of Passengers.		Stages.	Time Allowed.	Despatched from the General Post Office, the · of , 1837, at 8 p.m.
	In.	Out.	M. F.	H. M.	Coach No. ⌠With timepiece sent out ⌡ safe, No. to . Arrived at the Gloucester Coffee-House at .
Chaplin .			⌠12 2		Hounslow.
			{ 7 1	2 47	Staines.
			9 7		Bagshot. Arrived 10.47 p.m.
Company.			⌠ 9 1		Hartford Bridge.
			⎰10 1		Basingstoke.
			⎱ 8 0	2 54	Overton.
			3 5		Whitchurch. Arrived 1.41 a.m.
Broad . .			⌠ 6 7	0 39	Andover. Arrived 2.20 a.m.
			⌡13 7	1 19	Amesbury. Arrived 3.39 a.m.
Ward . .			9 5	0 55	Deptford Inn. Arrived 4.34 a.m.
Davis . .			⌠ 0 5	0 41	Wiley.
			⌡ 6 5		Chicklade. Arrived 5.15 a.m. (Bags dropped for Hindon, 1
Whitmash			⌠ 6 6		Mere. [mile distant.)
			⎰ 7 0	2 59	Wincanton.
			⎱13 4		Ilchester.
			4 1		Cart Gate. Arrived 8.14 a.m.
Jeffery .			⌠ 2 6		Water Gore, 6 miles from South Petherton.
				0 44	Bags dropped for that place.
			5 1		Ilminster. Arrived 8.58 a.m.
Soaring .			8 1	0 25	Breakfast 25 minutes. Dep. 9.23.
				0 46	Yarcombe, Heathfield Arms. Arrived 10.9 a.m.
Wheaton .			8 7	0 51	Honiton. Arrived 11 a.m.
Cockram .			⌠16 4	1 34	Exeter. Arrived 12.34 p.m.
				0 10	Ten minutes allowed.
			⎰10 3	1 57	Chudleigh.
			⎱ 9 3		Ashburton. Arrived 2.41 p.m.
Elliott . .			⌠13 2		Ivybridge.
			6 6		Bags dropped at Ridgway for Plympton, 3 furlongs distant.
			4 0	2 33	Plymouth. Arrived at the Post Office, Devonport, the : of
			1 7		, 1837, at 5.14 p.m. by timepiece. At by clock.
					Coach No. ⌠Delivered timepiece
			216 1	21 14	arr. . ⌡ safe, No. to .

The time of working each stage is to be reckoned from the coach's arrival, and as any lost time is to be recovered in the course of the stage, it is the coachman's duty to be as expeditious as possible, and to report the horse-keepers if they are not always ready when the coach arrives, and active in taking it off. The guard is to give his best assistance in changing, whenever his official duties do not prevent it.

By command of the Postmaster-General.

GEORGE LOUIS, *Surveyor and Superintendent.*

Fig 11 Timebill for the London–Exeter–Devonport (Quicksilver) Royal Mail, 1837

—speed limits, sober driving, giving way to the fastest vehicle, lighting up at fixed times. The Post Office approved of speed but not of 'speeding', but the natural hazards could not be forecast—fog, snow, flood, animals, and poor roads. The two primary elements in the progress of transport—greater speed and greater safety—can only be reconciled by genius, and no genius could improve on the stage coach and four horses.

What became of the coachmen? The *Times* in 1839 gave this answer: 'Steam, James Watt, and George Stephenson have a great deal to answer for. They will ruin the breed of horses, as they have already ruined the innkeepers and the coachmen, many of whom have already been obliged to seek relief at the poor house, or have died in penury and want.' Ruin and misery were wrought by the fast and sweeping changes brought about by the coming of the railways. Innkeepers, ostlers, post boys and stable helpers were all suddenly without occupation and means of livelihood. But what of the coachmen? Before the coming of the railways there were no less than 3,000 and very little is known of the fate of most of them—they just faded into obscurity. Some gloomily drove the omnibuses, despising them and living only in their recollection of days gone by. A few fortunate ones were taken into the service of some of the gentlemen who had ridden with them on the box seat in happier days. It is however on record that a number of guards transferred to the railway, where they became railway guards or did other duties.

Thomas Cross, who drove the Lynn Union for many years, sensing the winds of change, turned to writing. He wrote *The Autobiography of a Stage Coachman*, and in 1843 he published at Cambridge in pamphlet form verses in imitation of Gray's *Elegy*—'The Lament and Anticipation of a Stage Coachman'. It was extremely doleful and had sixteen pages of poetical effort; here are just two verses:

The smiling chambermaid, she too forlorn,

The boots, gruff voice, the waiter's busy jest,
The ostler's whistle, or the guard's loud horn,
No more shall call from their places of rest.

The next we heard some new-invented plan,
Had in Union lodged our ancient friend,
Come here and see, for thou shall see the man,
Doom'd by the railroad to so sad an end.

The Lynn Union was off the road in 1847 and Cross could not obtain any form of employment on the railway; he eked out a precarious existence on the occasional aid given him by the Norfolk squire Henry Villebois and others who had often been his passengers on his box seat. He published a number of verses, but he was not the poet he believed. He wrote a *History of Coaching* but in the bankruptcy of his printers the manuscript disappeared and so what might have been a valuable work was lost to posterity. He eventually found a home in Huggin's College, a charitable institution and lived to be eighty-six. A great number of ex-coachmen became inn-keepers and publicans; Ambrose Pickett of the Brighton Union & Item anticipated the end of coaching on the Brighton road in 1841 by becoming landlord of an inn in North Street, appropriately called the Coach & Horses. One of the more famous coachmen, Sam Hayward of the Shrewsbury Wonder, married a widow, the landlady of the Raven and Bell on Wyle Cop. But many were too ingrained in their old routines and could or would not take up new employments and subsisted on charity.

The rigours of their coaching days had in no way weakened them and many lived to ripe old ages. As each died he was reported as being supposedly the last. Some of these were Matthew Marsh of the Maidstone Times, died age ninety-four in 1887, William Clements, who drove the Tally Ho! and Eagle, died aged ninety-one in 1891. There was Philip (Tin) Carter, who drove the Red Rover on 19 June 1831 from

the Elephant & Castle to Brighton in 4hr 21min; it was the
occasion of the opening of William IV's first parliament and
he was delivering the King's Speech to Brighton. It was a
good advertisement for a new coach and he carried fourteen
passengers. Many record-making trips incidentally ran empty.

Again the last was Charles Ward who died at eighty-nine
on 9 December 1899; he was driving the Ipswich & Norwich
mail at Colchester at the age of seventeen. He later drove
the Devonport Quicksilver mail, moving then to the Brighton
day mail and for a time the Telegraph between Exeter and
Ilminster, a double journey of 66 miles. He was more busi-
nesslike than most and died the prosperous proprietor of
livery stables in the Brompton Road.

What became of the coachmen is partly answered by various
epitaphs. One such is that of Henry Skinner, who was killed
when his coach was upset at Middle Wallop on the Exeter
road. He was buried in Over Wallop churchyard and his
inscription is:

Sacred
to the memory of
HENRY SKINNER, a coachman,
who was killed near this place.
July 13th 1814
Aged 35 years.
With passengers of every age.
With care I drove from Stage to Stage,
Till deaths sad Hearse pass'd by unseen,
And stopt the course of my machine.

And a Latin inscription translated reads:

While I was conveying various passengers with the greatest skill, Black Death intervened—My machine is broken.

In South Shropshire, in St Lawrence's churchyard, Ludlow,

lies John Abingdon, who died in 1817, 'for forty years drove the Ludlow coach to London; a trusted servant, a careful driver, and an honest man'.

> His labour done, no more to town
> His onward course he bends;
> His teams unshut, his whips' laid up,
> And here his journey ends,
> Death locked his wheels and gave him rest,
> And never more to move,
> Till Christ shall call him with the blast
> To heavenly realms above.

The old whips had a whimsical way with them and sometimes a little pathos as well. The road was not only their profession but their passion, their whole life. Thus when a noted chaise driver at Lichfield, Jack Lewton, died in 1796, he was, at his last request, carried from the Bald Buck by six chaise drivers in scarlet jackets and buckskin breeches, the pall supported by six ostlers from the different inns. The funeral took place on 22 August in St Michael's churchyard, as near the turnpike road as possible; so that he might, as he said, enjoy the satisfaction of hearing his brother whips pass and repass.

By 1850 the era of coaching was over, its golden age being a short twenty-five years. So much had happened during the period from 1750 and it will be apparent that it served to establish our present way of life by facilitating movement and the communication of ideas. We started with an extract from *Pickwick Papers* and with another extract from this work we sadly bring this history to a close:

Now, in this piece of waste ground, there was, ... an enclosure belonging to some wheelwright who contracted with the Post Office for the purchase of the old worn out mail coaches; and my uncle, being very fond of coaches,

...took it into his head...to peep between the palings at these mails—about a dozen of which, he remembered to have seen, crowded together in a very forlorn and dismantled state, inside. My uncle...finding that he could not obtain a good peep between the palings, he got over them, and sitting himself quietly down on an old axle tree, began to contemplate the mail coaches with a great deal of gravity.

There might be a dozen of them, or there might be more—my uncle was never quite sure on this point, and being a man of very scrupulous veracity about numbers, didn't like to say—but there they stood, all huddled together in the most desolate condition imaginable. The doors had been torn from their hinges and removed; the linings had been stripped off: only a shred hanging here and there by a rusty nail; the lamps were gone, the poles had long since vanished, the iron work was rusty, the paint was worn away; the wind whistled through the chinks in the bare wood; and the rain, which had collected on the roofs, fell, drop by drop, into the insides with a hollow and melancholy sound. They were the decaying skeletons of departed mails, and in that lonely place, at that time of night, they looked chill and dismal.

My uncle rested his head upon his hands, and thought of the busy bustling people who had rattled about, years before, in the old coaches, and were now as silent and changed; he thought of the numbers of people to whom one of these crazy mouldering vehicles had borne, night after night, for many years, and through all weathers, the anxiously expected intelligence, the eagerly looked for remittance, the promised assurance of health and safety, the sudden announcement of sickness and death. The merchant, the lover, the wife, the widow, the mother, the schoolboy, the very child who tottered to the door at the postman's knock—how they had looked forward to the arrival of the old coach. And where were they all now?

APPENDICES

(From Harper's *Stage Coach and Mail in Days of Yore*)

1610 Patent granted for an Edinburgh–Leith waggon-coach.

1648 Southampton weekly stage mentioned.

1657 Stage-coaches introduced: the London–Chester Stage.

1658 First Exeter Stage.

1658 First York–Edinburgh Stage.

1661 First Oxford Stage.

1661 Glass windows first used in carriages—the Duke of York's carriage.

1662 Only six stage-coaches said to have been existing.

1665 Norwich Stage first mentioned.

1667 Bath Flying Machine established.

1667 London–Oxford coach in two days established.

1669 London–Oxford Flying Coach in one day established.

1673 Stages to York, Chester and Exeter advertised.

1679 London–Birmingham Stage by Banbury, mentioned.

1680 'Glass-coaches' mentioned.

1681 Stage-coaches became general: 119 in existence.

1706 London to York in four days.

1710 (about) Stage-coaches provided with glazed windows.

1730 'Baskets' or 'rumble-tumbles' introduced about this period.

1734 Teams of horses changed every day instead of coaches going to end of journey with same animals.

1734 Quick service advertised: Edinburgh to London in nine days.

1739 According to Pennant, gentlemen who were active horsemen still rode instead of going by coach.

1742 London to Oxford in two days.

1742 London to Birmingham, by Oxford in three days.

1751 London to Dover in one and a half days.

1753 Outsides carried on Shrewsbury Stage.

1754 London–Manchester Flying Coach in four and a half days.

1754 Springs to coaches first mentioned: the Edinburgh Stage.

1754 London–Edinburgh in ten days.

1758 London–Liverpool Flying Machine in three days.

1760 London–Leeds Flying Coach advertised in three days: took four.

1763 London–Edinburgh only once a month and in fourteen days.

1776 First duty on stage-coaches imposed.

1780 Stage-coaches become faster than post boys.

1782 Pennant describes contemporary travelling by light post-coaches as 'rapid journeys in easy chaises fit for the conveyance of soft inhabitants of Sylaris'.

1784 Mail-coach system established.

1800 (about) Fore- and hind-boots, framed to body of coach, became general.

1800 Coaches in general carry outside passengers.

1805 Springs under driving box introduced.

1819 'Patent Safety' coaches come into frequent use, to reassure travelling public alarmed by frequent accidents.

1824 Rise of the fast day-coaches: the Golden Age of coaching.

1824 Stockton–Darlington Railway opened: first beginnings of the railway era.

1830 Liverpool–Manchester Railway opened: coaching first seriously threatened.

1838 London–Birmingham Railway opened: first great blow to coaching: coaches taken off Holyhead road as far as Birmingham.

1839 Eastern Counties Railway opened to Chelmsford.

1840 Great Western Railway to Reading.

1840 London–Southampton Railway opened to Portsmouth: coaches taken off Portsmouth road.

1841 Great Western Railway opened to Bath and Bristol: coaches taken off Bath road.

1841 Brighton Railway opened: coaching ends on Brighton road.

1842 Last London–York Mail coach.

1844 Great Western Railway opened to Exeter: last coaches taken off Exeter road.

1845 Railways reach Norwich.

1845 Eastern Counties Railway opened to Cambridge.

1846 Edinburgh–Berwick Railway opened.

1847 East Anglian Railway opened to King's Lynn.

1848 Bedford Times, one of the last long-distance coaches, withdrawn.

1849 Shrewsbury–Birmingham Railway opened.

1850 Chester–Holyhead Railway opened.

1874 Last of the mail-coaches: the Thurso–Wick Mail gives place to the Highland Railway.

APPENDIX B:
SOME FORMER COACHING INNS STILL IN EXISTENCE AS HOTELS OR INNS

Ailsa Arms:	Girvan
Angel:	Abergavenny; Northampton
Angel & Royal:	Grantham
Beaufort Arms:	Monmouth
Bell:	Norwich; Sandwich; Saxmundham; Thetford
Beverley Arms:	Beverley
Black Swan:	Helmsley
Blue Boar:	Cambridge; Maldon
Bull:	Denbigh; Long Melford
Castle:	Conway; Ruthin; Windsor
Castle & Ball:	Marlborough
Church House Inn:	Torbryan, near Newton Abbot
County:	Taunton
Crown:	Amersham; Framlingham; Lynton; Woodbridge
Crown & Anchor:	Ipswich
Crown & Castle:	Orford
Crown Hotel & Posting House:	Bawtry
Cups:	Colchester
Dolphin:	Bovey Tracey; Southampton
Dolphin & Anchor:	Chichester
Dorset Arms:	East Grinstead
Duke's Head:	King's Lynn
Feathers:	Pocklington
Fleece:	Cirencester
Flying Horse:	Nottingham
Francis Hotel:	Bath
George:	Axminster; Cranbrook; Crawley; Hatherleigh; Huntingdon; Rye

George & Dragon:	Codicote
Golden Fleece:	Thirsk
Golden Lion:	Northallerton
Great White Horse:	Ipswich
Hoops Inn:	Horns Cross, Bideford
King's Arms:	Berkhamstead; Kingsbridge; Girvan
King's Head:	Conway; Monmouth
Langport Arms:	Langport
Lion:	Buckden; Shrewsbury
London:	Ottery St Mary
Luttrell Arms:	Dunster
Methuen Arms:	Corsham
Oxenham Arms:	South Zeal
Pembroke Arms:	Wilton
Pheasant Inn:	near Stockbridge
Radnorshire Arms:	Presteigne
Red Lion:	Colchester; Luton
Roebuck:	Buckhurst Hill
Rose & Crown:	Saffron Walden; Tonbridge
Royal Albion:	Broadstairs
Royal Castle:	Dartmouth
Royal Clarence:	Bridgwater; Exeter
Royal Fountain:	Sheerness
Royal Hotel:	Bideford; Llangollen; Purfleet, Ross on Wye
Royal Seven Stars:	Totnes
Saracen's Head:	Great Dunmow
Shakespeare Hotel:	Stratford on Avon
Speech House:	Forest of Dean
Suffolk Hotel:	Bury St Edmunds
Sun:	Hitchin
Swan:	Bibury; Harleston; Lavenham; Ross
The Swan:	Tewkesbury
Two Brewers:	Chipperfield
Warwick Arms:	Warwick

White Hart:	Braintree; Buckingham; Chipping Norton; Exeter; Newmarket; Salisbury; Spalding; Thetford
White Hart Royal:	Moreton in Marsh; Godstone
White Horse:	Dorking; Hertingfordbury; Moretonhampstead; Romsey
White Lion:	Eye
White Swan:	Stratford on Avon
Wynnstay Hotel:	Oswestry

APPENDIX C:
GLOSSARY OF COACHING TERMS

Butterflies:	short-distance public coach
Drag:	private four-in-hand coach
Flash of lightning:	glass of brandy or gin
Four-in-hand:	any coach drawn by a team of four horses
Leaders:	the foremost pair of horses in a team of four
Post boys:	men, not boys, of small size and light in weight attached to a posting inn. They acted as postillions, and when four horses were used for posting, two post boys mounted the nearside horses
Postillion:	a mounted groom or post boy who rode one of the horses harnessed to a coach. If an extra pair of leaders was added to a team of four, a postillion usually rode the nearside leader
Swallowing–Shadowing:	pocketing of short fares by guard, afterwards sharing with coachman
Skid-pan:	a metal plate which was attached to

	the near rear wheel when going down steep hills. Later coaches possessed, in addition, a 'pressure brake' which was operated by a hand lever or foot pedal
Splashing board:	the shield in front of the driver's seat
Stones:	the roads in built-up areas
Tiger:	a diminutive groom who travelled behind a private coach on a specially provided platform
Tommy:	a coachman's whip
Turn:	a section of good turnpike road
Wap-John:	private coachman
Wheelers:	the pair of horses nearest the coach in a team of more than two
Yellow-bounder:	a hired post-chaise, usually painted bright yellow

APPENDIX D:
MAIL COACHES DEPARTING FROM LONDON NIGHTLY IN 1836

Barton upon Humber (for Hull)
    Spread Eagle, Gracechurch St   W. Chaplin & Co
Birmingham and Stourport
    King's Arms, Snow Hill   J. Hearn & Co
Brighton
    Blossoms Inn, Laurence Lane   W. Gilbert & Co
Carmarthen
    Golden Cross, Charing Cross   B. W. Horne & Co
Devonport
    Swan with Two Necks, Lad Lane   W. Chaplin & Co
Dover
    Golden Cross, Charing Cross   B. W. Horne & Co

Edinburgh and Thurso
    Bull & Mouth, St Martins-le-Grand   E. Sherman & Co
Exeter
    Swan with Two Necks, Lad Lane/Bell &
    Crown, Holborn   W. Chaplin & Co/R. Fagg & Co
Falmouth (Quicksilver)
    Swan with Two Necks, Lad Lane   W. Chaplin & Co
Glasgow
    Bull & Mouth, St Martins-le-Grand   E. Sherman & Co
Halifax
    Golden Cross, Charing Cross   B. W. Horne & Co
Hastings
    Bolt in Tun, Fleet Street   R. Gray & Co
Holyhead
    Swan with Two Necks, Lad Lane   W. Chaplin & Co
Leeds
    Bull & Mouth, St Martins-le-Grand   E. Sherman & Co
Liverpool
    Swan with Two Necks, Lad Lane   W. Chaplin & Co
Louth
    Bell & Crown, Holborn   R. Fagg & Co
Norwich (via Newmarket)
    Belle Sauvage, Ludgate Hill   R. Nelson & Co
Norwich (via Ipswich)
    Spread Eagle, Gracechurch St   W. Chaplin & Co
Pembroke
    Swan with Two Necks, Lad Lane   W. Chaplin & Co
Penzance
    Bull & Mouth, St Martins-le-Grand   E. Sherman & Co
Portpatrick
    Swan with Two Necks, Lad Lane   W. Chaplin & Co
Portsmouth
    White Horse, Fetter Lane/Bolt in Tun,
    Fleet St   W. Chaplin & Co/R. Gray & Co

N

Poole
    Swan with Two Necks, Lad Lane   W. Chaplin & Co
Stroud
    Swan with Two Necks, Lad Lane   W. Chaplin & Co
Wells
    Swan with Two Necks, Lad Lane/Bell &
    Crown, Holborn (terminating
    alternately)   W. Chaplin & Co/R. Fagg & Co
Woodside (for Liverpool)
    Golden Cross, Charing Cross   B. W. Horne & Co
Yarmouth
    White Horse, Fetter Lane   W. Chaplin & Co

APPENDIX E:

MAIL AND STAGE COACHES SERVING LIVERPOOL IN 1836

London–Liverpool Royal Mail via Towcester, Newcastle-under-Lyme and Warrington	21hr 20min
London–Birkenhead (Woodside) Royal Mail via Northampton, Stafford, Nantwich and Chester	22hr 24min
Liverpool–Holyhead Royal Mail	
Liverpool–Lancaster Royal Mail	
Liverpool–Manchester Royal Mail	
Liverpool–Preston Royal Mail	
London–Liverpool via Birmingham and Chester (The Albion)	24hr
London–Liverpool via Warwick, Birmingham, Newcastle-under-Lyme and Warrington (The Express)	26hr
London–Liverpool via Northampton, Newcastle-under-Lyme and Warrington (The Umpire)	24hr
Liverpool–Aigburth	
Liverpool–Aintree	
Liverpool–Birmingham	

Liverpool–Cheltenham
Liverpool–Crosby Village
Liverpool–Fairfield Terrace
Liverpool–Kirkdale
Liverpool–Lancaster
Liverpool–Manchester
Liverpool–Ormskirk
Liverpool–Prescot
Liverpool–Preston
Liverpool–Railway Station
Liverpool–St Helens
Liverpool–Southport
Liverpool–Welshpool
Liverpool–Wigan
Liverpool–Woolton

(Mail coaches from their London inns at 7.30pm
and the Post Office at 8.00pm)

APPENDIX F:
MAIL AND STAGE COACHES SERVING EXETER IN 1836

London–Exeter Royal Mail via Salisbury and Shaftesbury	30hr 42min
London–Penzance Royal Mail via Salisbury, Exeter and Falmouth	37hr 50min
London–Falmouth (Quicksilver) Royal Mail via Amesbury, Exeter and Devonport	29hr 35min
Exeter–Budleigh Salterton Royal Mail	
Exeter–Dartmouth Royal Mail	
London–Exeter via Basingstoke, Amesbury, Wincanton and Ilminster (The Telegraph)	18hr
London–Exeter via Basingstoke, Amesbury, Wincanton and Ilminster (The Defiance)	19hr

London–Exeter via Basingstoke, Amesbury,
    Wincanton and Ilminster
    (The Exeter Subscription Coach)   19hr
London–Exeter via Basingstoke, Salisbury,
    Shaftesbury and Yeovil (The Traveller)   25hr
London–Exeter via Basingstoke, Salisbury,
    Shaftesbury and Yeovil (The Herald)   23hr
London–Devonport Royal Mail via Bath,
    Taunton and Exeter   27hr 5min
Exeter–Barnstaple
Exeter–Bideford
Exeter–Budleigh Salterton
Exeter–Cheltenham
Exeter–Dartmouth
Exeter–Devonport
Exeter–Exmouth
Exeter–Falmouth
Exeter–Sidmouth
Exeter–Southampton
Exeter–Teignmouth
Exeter–Tiverton
Exeter–Topsham
Exeter–Weymouth

(Mail coaches departed from their London inns at 7.30pm,
the Post Office at 8.00pm and, in the case of West Country
Mails, picked up passengers at the Gloucester Coffee House
shortly afterwards)

APPENDIX G:

MAIL AND STAGE COACHES SERVING NEWCASTLE UPON TYNE
IN 1836

Newcastle upon Tyne served by the London–

Edinburgh–Thurso Royal Mail	30hr 20min
London–Newcastle upon Tyne via Huntingdon, Grantham, Bawtry, Doncaster, York, Northallerton and Darlington (The Lord Wellington)	31hr

Newcastle upon Tyne–Alnwick
Newcastle upon Tyne–Barnard Castle
Newcastle upon Tyne–Bedlington
Newcastle upon Tyne–Berwick
Newcastle upon Tyne–Blaydon
Newcastle upon Tyne–Blythe
Newcastle upon Tyne–Carlisle
Newcastle upon Tyne–Durham
Newcastle upon Tyne–Edinburgh
Newcastle upon Tyne–Houghton-le-Spring
Newcastle upon Tyne–Leeds
Newcastle upon Tyne–Middleton
Newcastle upon Tyne–Morpeth
Newcastle upon Tyne–North Shields
Newcastle upon Tyne–Sunderland
Newcastle upon Tyne–Tynemouth
Newcastle upon Tyne–York

(Mail coaches departed from their London inns at 7.30pm
and the Post Office at 8.00pm)

APPENDIX H:

MAIL AND STAGE COACHES SERVING NORWICH IN 1836

London–Norwich Royal Mail via Bishop's Stortford and Newmarket	13hr 35min
London–Norwich Royal Mail via Ipswich	12hr 8min
Norwich–Cromer Royal Mail	

Norwich–Yarmouth Royal Mail

London–Norwich via Bishop's Stortford and Newmarket (The Magnet)	11hr
London–Norwich via Chelmsford and Bury St Edmunds (The Times)	13hr
London–Norwich via Chelmsford and Bury St Edmunds (The Phenomena)	13hr 30min
London–Norwich via Bishop's Stortford and Newmarket (The Telegraph)	12hr

Norwich–Bury St Edmunds
Norwich–Cromer
Norwich–East Dereham
Norwich–Halesworth
Norwich–Harleston
Norwich–Holt
Norwich–Litcham
Norwich–Lowestoft
Norwich–Lynn
Norwich–Newark
Norwich–North Walsham
Norwich–Stradbroke
Norwich–Watton
Norwich–Wells
Norwich–Yarmouth

(Mail coaches departed from their London inns at 7.30pm
and the Post Office at 8.00pm)

BIBLIOGRAPHY

Ash, Russell. *Discovering Highwaymen* (Tring 1970)
Baker, Margaret. *Discovering the Exeter Road* (Tring 1968)
Boswell's London Journal 1762–63 (repr 1966)
Bradley, Tom. *The Old Coaching Days in Yorkshire* (1889; repr 1968)
Bryant, Arthur. *Samuel Pepys: The Man in the Making* (repr 1967)
Copeland, John. *Roads and Their Traffic 1750–1850* (Newton Abbot 1968)
Corbett, E. *An Old Coachman's Chatter* (1890)
Dickens, Charles. *Pickwick Papers* (1836–7)
D'Orley, Alan A. *The Humber Ferries* (1968)
Ellis, Kenneth. *The Post Office in the Eighteenth Century* (Durham 1958)
Falmouth Corporation Official Guide Book
Harper, C. G. *Stage Coach and Mail in Days of Yore* (1903)
Henderson, J. *Firearms Collecting for Amateurs* (1966)
Hindley, Geoffrey. *A History of Roads* (1971)

Keverne, Richard. *Tales of Old Inns* (1948)

Marsh Edwards, J. C. 'The Tantivy Trot on the Brighton Road', *Sussex Life*

Morgan, G. B. *General View of the Agriculture of the County of Cornwall* (1811)

Newberry Cox. *Reminiscences of Forty Years Spent as Postmaster of Falmouth* (private notes)

Noall, Cyril. *A History of Cornish Mail and Stage Coaches.* D. Bradford Burton (Truro 1963)

Norway, Arthur. *History of the Post Office Packet Service*

Robinson, A. W. *A History of the Ship Letters of the British Isles* (1955)

Soultry, R. *Early Tours in Devon and Cornwall, Letter from England* (1802)

Speakman, R. *Transport in Yorkshire* (1969)

Strong, L. A. G. *The Rolling Road* (1956)

Thomas, J. M. *Roads before the Railways (1750–1851), History at Source*

ACKNOWLEDGEMENTS

THE AUTHORS wish to express their appreciation of the assistance received from the staffs of Kingston upon Hull Museum of Transport; Kingston upon Hull City library; the North Ferriby branch of the East Riding County library; Falmouth public library; and the Post Office Headquarters, St Martins-le-Grand, London. Also George Darley who rebuilt the Hero, Ian Milligan of National Travel (NBC) Ltd, Iain Macauley of Charlecote Carriages, Ida Payne of Trust House Forte Ltd and Jack Winn who drew the sketches of the coaches. Several of the illustrations are from old prints and where the source is known this is acknowledged. We have endeavoured to obtain illustrations depicting preserved coaches and other items of the coaching era and we are grateful for the help we have received in this direction. We have been much inspired by the works of Charles Dickens from which we have quoted. Coaching has almost a literature of its own and the bibliography lists a number of works which amplify those matters to which we have only been able to give brief attention. In particular we would mention *Roads and their Traffic 1750–1850* by John Copeland and *Directory of Stage Coach Services 1836* compiled by Alan Bates. It takes all the latter book to list the services running in 1836, and we have extracted details for four cities to illustrate the excellent coverage of services. We have sorted through much data, a considerable amount conflicting, and if there are any errors then we hasten to apologise.

R. and J.A.

Index